The Elephant and the Cassowary

Ruskin Bond has been writing for over sixty years, and now has over 120 titles in print—novels, collections of short stories, poetry, essays, anthologies and books for children. His first novel, *The Room on the Roof*, received the prestigious John Llewellyn Rhys Prize in 1957. He has also received the Padma Shri (1999), the Padma Bhushan (2014) and two awards from Sahitya Akademi—one for his short stories and another for his writings for children. In 2012, the Delhi government gave him its Lifetime Achievement Award.

Born in 1934, Ruskin Bond grew up in Jamnagar, Shimla, New Delhi and Dehradun. Apart from three years in the UK, he has spent all his life in India, and now lives in Mussoorie with his adopted family.

The Elephant and the Cassowary

Selected and Compiled by
RUSKIN BOND

Published by
Rupa Publications India Pvt. Ltd 2017
7/16, Ansari Road, Daryaganj
New Delhi 110002

Sales centres:
Allahabad Bengaluru Chennai
Hyderabad Jaipur Kathmandu
Kolkata Mumbai

Copyright © Ruskin Bond 2017

This is a work of fiction. Names, characters, places and incidents are either the product of the author's imagination or are used fictitiously and any resemblance to any actual person, living or dead, events or locales is entirely coincidental.

All rights reserved.
No part of this publication may be reproduced, transmitted, or stored in a retrieval system, in any form or by any means, electronic, mechanical, photocopying, recording or otherwise, without the prior permission of the publisher.

ISBN: 978-81-291-4649-6

First impression 2017

10 9 8 7 6 5 4 3 2 1

Printed at Thomson Press India Ltd., Faridabad

This book is sold subject to the condition that it shall not, by way of trade or otherwise, be lent, resold, hired out, or otherwise circulated, without the publisher's prior consent, in any form of binding or cover other than that in which it is published.

CONTENTS

Introduction	*vii*
The Falcon and I	1
Jean George	
Rikki-Tikki-Tavi	10
Rudyard Kipling	
The Haunts of Isabeline	29
C.H. Donald	
The Elephant and the Cassowary	49
Ruskin Bond	
The Pale One	52
John Eyton	
Hunting with a Camera	65
F.W. Champion	
The Life of a Tiger	74
S. Eardley-Wilmot	
The Man-Eater of Botta Singarum	80
Henry Astbury Leveson	
The Eye of the Eagle	87
Ruskin Bond	

The Tiger and the Terrier *Brig. General R.G. Burton*	97
Toomai of the Elephants *Rudyard Kipling*	103
Down Elephant Street *K.M. Eady*	125

INTRODUCTION

The lure of the jungle with its thick canopies, waterholes and grasslands. The call of the birds, the warning cries of the monkeys, the sudden stillness. The astonishment on spotting a rare bird or reptile, the eternal wait of wildlife enthusiasts in Indian forests—a viewing of the mighty tiger. Experiences in jungles can become almost like an addiction for many. There are those who seem to come to life only when they are in the embrace of the forests. Outside of them, they wilt and pine.

Well, not all of us can visit the forests as much as we want to. I have been to a number of them, staying nights in forest rest houses and venturing forth on elephant back or in jeeps for safaris. And when night fell, and the forest guards had made sure that we were tucked in after feeding us simple but tasty meals, I wandered to forgotten bookcases and pulled out old copies of railway magazines.

Many such journals carried accounts of those who had ventured into the forests, either to survey or as shikaris and then wrote of their experiences. There was a time when shikar was acceptable as a sport or for commercial reasons or for protection. The walls of old houses lined with mounted heads and horns were a common sight. That helped in decimating the wildlife population, particularly of large predators like tigers and lions. As a boy, I have been part of hunting expeditions, when I chose to spend most of the time in the bungalow.

To my delight, there have been times when the group that set forth into the forest had to make a hasty retreat due to a run-in with a hive of bees or a nest of red ants.

In this book, I have gathered some stories about wild animals. There are a few about birds too. All of them make for fascinating reading, whether they are fiction or fact. 'The Falcon and I' is a story of a young woman's own gradual acceptance of the limits that are set for her by society while she trains a fierce falcon into submission. It's a sad and poignant fact that domesticated creatures are made to lose much of their innate instincts because it suits us humans. I have included two stories by that great chronicler of animal lore—Rudyard Kipling. His stories featuring animals and humans are replete with drama and insights into human nature. My story 'The Elephant and the Cassowary' is about two mismatched animals who lived once in our home and their encounters with each other.

To read about the jungle and animals when written about by a person who knows and loves them is a delightful experience. F.W. Champion was one such person. He was in the Indian Forest Service and spent much time in the forests with his camera. He wrote about his experiences in books that reveal his deep knowledge of forests. Included here is his account of 'shooting' a tigress. It's clearly the kind of shooting that he prefers and I particularly like the last lines from his essay:

> ...she lives on and may still provide us with harmless pleasure, so who can say that, once we have overcome our primitive and savage lust of killing, hunting with a camera is not the peer of any form of blood-hunting that the world can produce.

Ruskin Bond

THE FALCON AND I

Jean George

I was alone in the attic. My children were off to school. The sweep of my broom was checked by an object behind the trunk; the old wooden box that held my girlhood diaries. Amused, I lifted a blue-leather one from the lot and opened it. I don't remember cleaning the rest of the attic. For the words I read startled me with intimations that were not there when I had written: 'I spoke to my beloved falcon tonight, and I said to him: "If there is a way to balance our wings on the sky we shall go that way together."'

At thirteen I had had no other thought than that I adored the bird my twin brothers had given me. But these many years later those words crystallized my relationship with the falcon. We *had* balanced our wings together, for I had turned the wild, noble bird into a disciplined hunter precisely during the period when I myself was being groomed for womanhood. And there in the attic I began to understand for the first time the subtle ways in which the falcon and I grew up together, learning through passionate rebellion and quiet acceptance that freedom begins only when necessary restrictions are buried in habit.

I first saw the young sparrow hawk in the bottom of a bushel basket in our kitchen. He flopped on his back and, eyes flashing, threatened me with his open talons. He looked ferocious—until a wisp of the natal down he was shedding landed comically on the end of his hooked beak. 'He's wonderful!' I exclaimed, as my hand circled his steely-blue body. He cried 'killie' in rage, and I winced as he dug his needle talons into my hand. Weeping and laughing, I pried the talons out of my flesh and pressed the hot, woodsy-smelling creature against my cheek. 'You are only four weeks old and have a lot to learn,' I whispered with great sadness, for only that morning my own nestlinghood had come to an end. My mother had finished telling me the facts of life.

My brothers, three years my senior and already knowledgeable falconers with hawks of their own, were both amused and pleased with the meeting of girl and bird. 'The sparrow hawk is a noble bird,' said my brother John. 'It is one of the smallest of the true falcons, or noble birds of prey.'

'And the training,' my brother Frank added solemnly, 'must begin immediately. Feed the falcon nothing—and I mean nothing—unless he takes it from your hand. Use this whistle'—he gave three notes—'then let him eat.'

I was left alone with the young and the noble. I tried to make the bird sit on my hand. He bit a finger. I stroked him. He flew at my face. There and then I named him Bad Boy.

All afternoon I tried to win him with succulent grasshoppers. He looked at them and screamed in hunger, but he would not take them from my hand. I cried. Then came a constricting fear: The little falcon would die of starvation right before my eyes! In desperation I threw him a grasshopper. Bad Boy stared in anger; then a yellow foot shot out and snagged the morsel. The bird wolfed. Certain that he would be won by my generosity, I reached out to take hire. But he snapped at me and ran under the radiator. From there he fought my hand with such ferocity that it bled. John and Frank found me there, crying, and brought the gladiator out with gauntlets. Then I confessed what I had done.

'Now you musn't feed him anything until tomorrow. When he is hungry enough he *will* eat from your hand.'

That night I resolved in my diary to 'do it right—it will be less heartbreaking in the long run.' The wisdom to 'do it right' had stemmed from an earlier experience—when I'd spent a dollar and declared I hadn't. Supporting one untruth with another had become so agonisingly complicated that when I finally told the truth it was so simple I was startled. Alone there in the attic I saw that I had transferred that experience to the bird: It *was* easier—in the long run—to follow the rules.

I turned a page of the diary. It reported that I got up at 5 a.m. Bad Boy was still in his temporary home, the bushel basket. When he saw me he again bristled for a fight, bill open and talons exposed. But when I whistled the call that was to mean, 'Come, food,' and held out a grasshopper, his feathers relaxed and he nibbled tentatively at the grasshopper—then began to eat! I slipped my finger under his feet and lifted him out of the basket. Trembling, I fed him two, three, four grasshoppers. When he was done he was still perched on my hand. Quickly I apologized to the bird for the training. I remember explaining that it would get worse before it got better. 'It is being done so that when you fly free you will know what you are doing,' I wrote in my diary. Reading the words now, I was not sure whether they were addressed to the falcon or to myself One day, noting that Bad Boy's wings had filled out to their full span, my brothers said: 'It is time to put leg straps on him—falconers call them jesses—for now that he can fly you must have control of him.'

On the kitchen table we cut the jesses, two slender strips of soft deer hide. An ingenious falconer's knot held the straps to the legs. Frank deftly put the jesses on Bad Boy, and I flipped him to my wrist, holding the straps. Bad Boy tried to fly, fell forward, tried to fly again and sat still. We snapped a leash to the jesses by a swivel designed to keep the leash from twisting or binding the bird. Then we took him out to the perch waiting for him and tied the leash to a circle of wire at the base of the pole. He hopped to his perch, bobbed his head, blinked his eyes and immediately tried to fly away. Apparently surprised when he was pulled back, he flopped and screamed at the end of the cord. Then presently he flew back to his perch and sat there quietly.

That night my first social-dancing lesson began. Over our loud protest, the neighbourhood mothers had hired an instructor to teach their boys and girls. The frightened group gathered in our living room, and as my first partner put his arm self-consciously around my waist I suddenly remembered that I had not checked Bad Boy—he might be tangled in his new leash. I ran! When I returned I could hear the teacher droning on and on, 'Step-together-step.' I can still see that roomful of young adolescents—step-together-step, step-together-step. A boy breaks away to see if he can jump and touch the chandelier—step-together-step. A girl gets the giggles and has to get a drink of water—step-together-step. And next morning, when I forced Bad. Boy to come halfway across the yard for food, the words passed my lips: 'Step-together-step.' The reluctant bird circled on his perch and 'killied' for fifteen minutes—but in the end he, too, accepted the strange new rules.

Every summer our family vacationed in my father's old home in the Pennsylvania mountains. There, in the enormous mid-Victorian house we shared with cousins, aunts and uncles, I was trained in cooking, sewing, housekeeping. And there Bad Boy became a falcon—a hunter. A few weeks after our arrival, my brothers informed me that Bad Boy was trained well enough to fly free, which meant I should take his leash off when I whistled him to my hand. 'Don't feed him for a day,' Frank told me. 'Then try him out.'

From the beginning there was something 'off' about that day. Mother was upset with me because I had come down the rainspout instead of the steps. She thought I was too big for such displays—'undignified' she called it, using the word I resented so terribly. Added to that was my apprehension about flying the falcon free. If I lost that bird, my uncertain world would collapse. For I was truly happy, it seemed to me, only when I was with him. To console the hungry Bad Boy, I kept him company that afternoon, reading under the maple tree near his perch. But he kept begging me for food, and when I could stand it no longer I caught several crickets and fed them to him. He flapped his wings ecstatically.

The next morning I dared not confess to my brothers what I had done, so we prepared for the flight. John unsnapped the leash. I stood at the end of the long yard with the lure—a wooden block on a string, covered with feathers to look like a bird, on which food was tied. I whistled and waved the lure. The falcon sped down the yard, missed the lure and headed for the open sky. For the moment I was left breathless by his mastery of the air. His wings folded, spread, clipped the winds. He rode them higher and higher—and then he was gone.

John, Frank and I spelled each other all day in search. Night came. The perch under the maple tree was still vacant.

I cried all night. At dawn I heard the familiar 'killie, killie, killie'. I dashed down the steps and there, on his perch, I found Bad Boy—lifting his wings and turning as if the leash were still snapped to the jesses! I fought down the impulse to run to him. I moved forward with great restraint. When I was two feet away, he jumped to my shoulder and pecked my chin—hard. He was *hungry*. When he was safely leashed I took the .22 rifle and brought down a house sparrow near the barn. On the run I went back to the falcon and unsnapped his leash. I walked to the end of the yard and, holding out the sparrow, whistled. He dropped onto his wings, swooped over, the grass and hit my hand with a blow—exactly the way a trained falcon should. Needless to say, my brothers were awakened early that morning.

Bird and I sailed on smoothly from that day. He needed only to hear me whistle and he was on my shoulder or the lure. Even when I returned to school, with the blooming of the goldenrod, Bad Boy accepted my absence with, no backsliding in his discipline.

But there was backsliding in *my* training. Mother came to my room with a package one night, while I was getting ready for bed. She looked at me as woman to woman, and a knowing warmth softened her face. 'You are developing nicely,' she said and, to underline the alarming truth, opened the package—a girdle, silk stockings and a brassiere! I wanted to run, hide, drop dead—anything to escape—and after she left I, buried them resentfully at the bottom of the bureau drawer like a guilty secret. In the following months several occasions arose when I should have worn them, and didn't. But Mother said nothing more than that my brothers seemed to be able to wear neckties now without grumbling.

One day I came home late from school to find my brothers

on the back steps amid a clutter of tools, leather and patterns. We're going to hood Bad Boy,' Frank explained.

'Oh, no!' I protested. 'It's cruel. He won't be able to see.'

'Well, you're too busy to keep him in training. He's getting wild, breaking his tail feathers pulling at the leash. A hood will keep him quiet.'

The completed hood was handsome, decorated with a topknot of chicken feathers and with a clever drawstring that could be easily tightened or loosened. I would not go with them to hood my bird, but I watched from the back porch. Confident that he would not tolerate this abuse, I waited for him to fly into a fury, to fight back. But Bad Boy stopped screaming the moment the hood was on. He shook it, scratched it violently, then sat quietly in the sudden night. As good falconers, John and Frank intended that Bad Boy should be hooded when not hunting. But I could not bear the thought of my sky-loving bird sitting in darkness. I unhooded him and took him to my room. If I was too busy to keep him in training, then I would make a pet of him. And Bad Boy as a pet—although a breach of falconry rules—was a satisfying arrangement for me. He sat on my head or the back of my chair while I studied. And when there was company, he always caused such a sensation flying around the house that I forgot my own awkward embarrassment in the midst of adults.

One evening my father was having a colleague to dinner, and by the preparations under way I knew Mother wanted me to look particularly nice. I went to my room and dug out those hidden garments. Shyly I put them on, and when I was dressed I remember standing a moment at the door. An exciting pride came over me. I turned back to Bad Boy. But this time, instead of whistling him to my shoulder, I slipped the hood over his head and watched the calm descend, with some vague understanding that the hood wasn't so cruel after all. The mention of this in my diary was brief: 'It's not scary at all,' I wrote, and walked calmly downstairs. My need for the falcon seems to have ended here.

The following summer Bad Boy was so tame that he was rarely leashed. He would go out to the meadows to catch his own food and bring it back to his perch to eat. I began to notice, however, that each time he went he stayed away longer. Once, as he winged over my head, I whistled and called in vain. When night came I saw him huddled against the chimney for warmth, so I crawled out on the roof and got him. Not long afterward Bad Boy was gone for three days, then a week.

He came back to the chimney a wild bird. I climbed up to get him but he flew away from me. Leaning against the chimney, watching him spurn me, I suddenly didn't want it to end like this. There was something so final, at once sad and exciting, about the parting. I could smell the bricks through my sobs. 'Did I know then,' I said to myself in the attic, 'that those tears *were* for the farewell to my childhood?' I recall having been a little surprised that I was not more upset over the absences of my falcon.

But other things were clamouring for attention—canoeing races on the creek, baseball games, campfire picnics. Then one day, when he had been gone two weeks, I came home to find a yellow gown on my bed, so romantically bouffant it took my breath away. Holding it up to myself I looked dreamily into my mirror. Suddenly a movement in the mirror caught my eye. Bad Boy was in the tree outside my window, looking at me. I could get him by merely stepping out on the roof. I would—but first I turned slowly before the mirror, admiring the dress. When I had completed the circle, the falcon was gone. I ran to the window and I could see his pointed wings against the sky as he circled the chimney, the house, the yard. Then he turned and flew like a wild bird. This time, I sensed, he would not be back

I dropped my head in the yellow organdy and waited for the tears. They did not come. In the blue-leather diary I wrote: 'Now you belong to the sky—good-bye, my pretty friend. How different the winds that carry us will be.'

The falcon and I were free.

RIKKI-TIKKI-TAVI

Rudyard Kipling

At the hole where he went in
Red-Eye called to Wrinkle-Skin.
hear what little Red-Eye saith:
Nag, come up and dance with death!

Eye to eye and head to head,
   (Keep the measure, Nag.)
This shall end when one is dead;
   (At the pleasure, Nag.)
Turn for turn and twist for twist
   (Run and hide thee, Nag.)
Hah! The hooded Death has missed!
   (Woe betide thee, Nag!)

This is the story of the great war that Rikki-tikki-tavi fought single-handed, through the bathrooms of the big bungalow in Segowlee cantonment. Darzee, the tailor-bird, helped him, and Chuchundra, the musk-rat, who never comes out into the middle of the floor, but always creeps round by the wall, gave him advice: but Rikki-tikki did the real fighting.

He was a mongoose, rather like a little cat in his fur and his tail, but quite like a weasel in his head and his habits. His eyes and the end of his restless nose were pink; he could scratch himself anywhere he pleased, with any leg, front or back, that he chose to use; he could fluff up his tail till it looked like a bottlebrush, and his war-cry as he scuttled through the long grass, was 'Rikk-tikk-tikki-tikki-tchk!'

One day, a high summer flood washed him out of the burrow where he lived with his father and mother, and carried him, kicking and clucking down a roadside ditch. He found a little wisp of grass floating there, and clung to it till he lost his senses. When he revived, he was lying in the hot sun on the middle of a garden path, very draggled indeed, and a small boy was saying, 'Here's a dead mongoose. Let's have a funeral'.

'No,' said his mother; 'let's take him in and dry him. Perhaps he isn't really dead.' They took him into the house, and a big man picked him up between his finger and thumb and said he was not dead but half-choked; so they wrapped him in cotton-wool, and warmed him, and he opened his eyes and sneezed.

'Now,' said the big man (he was an Englishman who had just moved into the bungalow); 'don't frighten him, and we'll see what he'll do.'

It is the hardest thing in the world to frighten a mongoose, because he is eaten up from nose to tail with curiosity. The motto of all the mongoose family is, 'Run and find out'; and Rikki-tikki was a true mongoose. He looked at the cotton-wool, decided that it was not good to eat, ran all round the table, sat up and put his fur in order, scratched himself, and jumped on the small boy's shoulder.

'Don't be frightened, Teddy,' said his father. 'That's his way of making friends.'

'Ouch! He's tickling under my chin,' said Teddy.

Rikki-tikki looked down between the boy's collar and neck, snuffed at his ear, and climbed down to the floor, where he sat rubbing his nose.

'Good gracious,' said Teddy's mother, 'and that's a wild creature! I suppose he's so tame because we've been kind to him.'

'All mongooses are like that,' said her husband. 'If Teddy doesn't pick him up by the tail, or try to put him in a cage, he'll run in and out of the house all day long. Let's give him something to eat.'

They gave him a little piece of raw meat. Rikki-tikki liked it immensely, and when it was finished he went out into the veranda and sat in the sunshine and fluffed up his fur to make it dry to the roots. Then he felt better. 'There are more things to find out about in this house,' he said to himself, 'than all my family could find out in all their lives. I shall certainly stay and find out.'

He spent all that day roaming over the house. He nearly drowned himself in the bathtubs, put his nose into the ink on a writing-table, and burned it on the end of the big man's cigar, for he climbed up in the big man's lap to see how writing was done. At nightfall he ran into Teddy's nursery to watch how kerosene lamps were lighted, and when Teddy went to bed Rikki-tikki climbed up too; but he was a restless companion, because he had to get up and attend to every noise all through the night, and find out what made it. Teddy's mother and father came in, the last thing, to look at their boy, and Rikki-tikki was awake on the pillow.

'I don't like that,' said Teddy's mother; 'he may bite the child.'

'He'll do no such thing,' said the father. 'Teddy's safer with that little beast than if he had a bloodhound to watch him. If a snake came into the nursery now—' But Teddy's mother wouldn't think of anything so awful.

Early in the morning Rikki-tikki came to early breakfast in the veranda riding on Teddy's shoulder, and they gave him banana and some boiled egg; and he sat on all their laps one after the other because a well-brought-up mongoose always hopes to be a house-mongoose some day and have rooms to run about in, and Rikki-tikki's mother (she used to live in the General's house at Segowlee) had carefully told Rikki what to do if ever he came across white men.

Then Rikki-tikki went out into the garden to see what was to be seen. It was a large garden, only half cultivated, with bushes as big as summer-houses of Marshal Niel roses, lime and orange trees, clumps of bamboos, and thickets of high grass. Rikki-tikki licked his lips. 'This is a splendid hunting-ground,' he said, and his tail grew bottle-brushy at the thought of it, and he scuttled up and down the garden, snuffing here and there till he heard very sorrowful voices in a thorn-bush. It was Darzee, the tailor-bird, and his wife. They had made a beautiful nest by pulling two big leaves together and stitching up the edges with fibres; they had filled the hollow with cotton and downy fluff. The nest swayed to and fro, as they sat on the rim and cried.

'What is the matter?' asked Rikki-tikki.

'We are very miserable,' said Darzee, 'One of our babies fell out of the nest yesterday and Nag ate him.'

'H'm!' said Rikki-tikki, 'that is very sad—but I am a stranger here. Who is Nag?'

Darzee and his wife only cowered down in the nest without answering, for from the thick grass at the foot of the bush there came a low hiss—a horrid cold sound that made Rikki-tikki jump back two clear feet. Then inch by inch out of the grass rose up the head and spread hood of Nag, the big black cobra, and he was five feet long from tongue to tail. When he had lifted one-third of himself clear off the ground, he stayed balancing to and fro exactly as a dandelion-tuft balances in the wind, and he looked at Rikki-tikki with the wicked snake's eyes that never change their expression, whatever the snake may be thinking of.

'Who is Nag?' he said. 'I am Nag. The great god Brahma put his mark upon all our people when the first cobra spread his hood to keep the sun off Brahma as he slept. Look, and be afraid!'

He spread out his hood more than ever, and Rikki-tikki saw the spectacle-mark on the back of it that looks exactly like the eye part of a hook-and-eye fastening. He was afraid for a minute; but it is impossible for a mongoose to stay frightened for any length of time, and though Rikki-tikki had never met a live cobra before, his mother had fed him on dead ones, and he knew that it was a grown mongoose's business in life to fight and eat snakes. Nag knew that too, and at the bottom of his cold heart he was afraid.

'Well,' said Rikki-tikki, and his tail began to fluff up again, 'marks or no marks, do you think it is right for you to eat fledglings out of a nest?'

Nag was thinking to himself, and watching the least little movement in the grass behind Rikki-tikki. He knew that mongooses in the garden meant death sooner or later for him and his family; but he wanted to get Rikki-tikki off his guard. So he dropped his head a little, and put it on one side.

'Let us talk,' he said. 'You eat eggs. Why should I not eat birds?'

'Behind you! Look behind you!' sang Darzee. Rikki-tikki knew better than to waste time in staring. He jumped up in the air as high as he could go, and just under him whizzed by the head of Nagaina, Nag's wicked wife. She had crept up behind him as he was talking, to make an end of him; and he heard her savage hiss as the stroke missed. He came down almost across her back, and if he had been an old mongoose he would have known that then was the time to break her back with one bite; but he was afraid of the terrible lashing return-stroke of the cobra. He bit, indeed, but did not bite long enough, and he jumped clear of the whisking tail, leaving Nagaina torn and angry.

'Wicked, wicked Darzee!' said Nag, lashing up as high as he could reach toward the nest in the thorn-bush; but Darzee had built it out of reach of snakes, and it only swayed to and fro.

Rikki-tikki felt his eyes growing red and hot (when a mongoose's eyes grow red, he is angry), and he sat back on his tail and hind legs like a little kangaroo, and looked all around him, and chattered with rage. But Nag and Nagaina had disappeared into the grass. When a snake misses its stroke, it never says anything or gives any sign of what it means to do next. Rikki-tikki did not care to follow them, for he did not feel sure that he could manage two snakes at once. So he trotted off to the gravel path near the house, and sat down to think. It was a serious matter for him.

If you read the old books of natural history, you will find they say that when the mongoose fights the snake and happens to get bitten, he runs off and eats some herb that cures him. That is not true. The victory is only a matter of quickness of eye and quickness of foot—snake's blow against mongoose's jump—and as no eye can follow the motion of a snake's head when it strikes, that makes things much more wonderful than any magic herb. Rikki-tikki knew he was a young mongoose, and it made him all the more pleased to think that he had managed to escape a blow from behind. It gave him confidence in himself, and when Teddy came running down the path, Rikki-tikki was ready to be petted.

But just as Teddy was stooping, something flinched a little in the dust, and a tiny voice said, 'Be careful. I am death!' It was Karait, the dusty brown snakeling that lies for choice on the dusty earth; and his bite is as dangerous as the cobra's. But he is so small that nobody thinks of him, and so he does the more harm to people.

Rikki-tikki's eyes grew red again, and he danced up to Karait with the peculiar rocking, swaying motion that he had inherited from his family. It looks very funny, but it is so perfectly balanced a gait that you can fly off from it at any angle you please; and in dealing with snakes this is an advantage. If Rikki-tikki had only known, he was doing a much more dangerous thing than fighting Nag, for Karait is so small, and can turn so quickly, that unless Rikki bit him close to the back of the head, he would get the return-stroke in his eye or lip. But Rikki did not know: his eyes were all red, and he rocked back and forth, looking for a good place to hold. Karait struck out. Rikki jumped sideways and tried to run in, but the wicked little dusty grey head lashed within a fraction of his shoulder, and he had to jump over the body, and the head followed his heels close.

Teddy shouted to the house, 'Oh, look here! Our mongoose is killing a snake'; and Rikki-tikki heard a scream from Teddy's mother. His father ran out with a stick, but by the time he came up, Karait had lunged out once too far, and Rikki-tikki had sprung, jumped on the snake's back, dropped his head far between his forelegs, bitten as high up the back as he could get hold, and rolled away. The bite paralysed Karait, and Rikki-tikki was just going to eat him up from the tail, after the custom of his family at dinner, when he remembered that a full meal makes a slow mongoose, and if he wanted all his strength and quickness ready, he must keep himself thin.

He went away for a dust-bath under the castor-oil bushes, while Teddy's father beat the dead Karait. 'What is the use of that?' thought Rikki-tikki. 'I have settled it all'; and then Teddy's mother picked him up from the dust and hugged him, crying that he had saved Teddy from death, and Teddy's father said that he was a providence, and Teddy looked on with big scared eyes. Rikki-tikki was rather amused at all the fuss, which, of course, he did not understand. Teddy's mother might just as well have petted Teddy for playing in the dust. Rikki was thoroughly enjoying himself.

That night, at dinner, walking to and fro among the wineglasses on the table, he could have stuffed himself three times over with nice things; but he remembered Nag and Nagaina, and though it was very pleasant to be patted and petted by Teddy's mother, and to sit on Teddy's shoulder, his eyes would get red from time to time, and he would go off into his long war-cry of 'Rikk-tikk-tikki-tikki-tchk!'

Teddy carried him off to bed, and insisted on Rikki-tikki sleeping under his chin. Rikki-tikki was too well bred to bite or scratch, but as soon as Teddy was asleep he went off for his nightly walk round the house, and in the dark he ran up against Chuchundra, the musk-rat, creeping round by the wall. Chuchundra is a broken-hearted little beast. He whimpers and cheeps all the night, trying to make up his mind to run into the middle of the room, but he never gets there.

'Don't kill me,' said Chuchundra, almost weeping. 'Rikki-tikki, don't kill me.'

'Do not a think a snake-killer kills musk-rats?' said Rikki-tikki scornfully.

'Those who kill snakes get killed by snakes,' said Chuchundra, more sorrowfully than ever. And how am I to be sure that Nag won't mistake me for you some dark night?'

'There's not the least danger,' said Rikki-tikki; 'but Nag is in the garden, and I know you don't go there.'

'My cousin Chua, the rat, told me—' said Chuchundra, and then he stopped.

'Told you what?'

'H'sh! Nag is everywhere, Rikki-tikki. You should have talked to Chua in the garden.'

'I didn't—so you must tell me. Quick, Chuchundra, or I'll bite you!'

Chuchundra sat down and cried till the tears rolled off his whiskers. 'I am a very poor man,' he sobbed. 'I never had spirit enough to run out into the middle of the room. H'sh! I mustn't tell you anything. Can't you *hear*, Rikki-tikki?'

Rikki-tikki listened. The house was as still as still, but he thought he could just catch the faintest *scratch-scratch* in the world—a noise as faint as that of wasp walking on a windowpane—the dry scratch of a snake's scales on brickwork.

'That's Nag or Nagaina,' he said to himself; 'and he is crawling into the bathroom sluice. You're right, Chuchundra; I should have talked to Chua.'

He stole off to Teddy's bathroom, but there was nothing there, and then to Teddy's mother's bathroom. At the bottom of the smooth plaster wall there was a brick pulled out to make a sluice for the bath-water, and as Rikki-tikki stole in by the masonry curb where the bath is put, he heard Nag and Nagaina whispering together outside in the moonlight.

'When the house is emptied of people,' said Nagaina to her husband, 'he will have to go away, and then the garden will be our own again. Go in quietly, and remember that the big man who killed Karait is the first one to bite. Then come out and tell me, and we will hunt for Rikki-tikki together.'

'But are you sure that there is anything to be gained by killing the people?' said Nag.

'Everything. When there were no people in the bungalow, did we have any mongoose in the garden? So long as the bungalow is empty, we are king and queen of the garden; and remember that as soon as our eggs in the melon-bed hatch (as they may tomorrow), our children will need room and quiet.'

'I had not thought of that,' said Nag. I will go, but there is no need that we should hunt for Rikki-tikki afterward. I will kill the big man and his wife, and the child if I can, and come away quietly. Then the bungalow will be empty, and Rikki-tikki will go.'

Rikki-tikki tingled all over with rage and hatred at this, and then Nag's head came through the sluice, and his five feet of cold body followed it. Angry as he was, Rikki-tikki was very frightened as he saw the size of the big cobra. Nag coiled himself up, raised his head, and looked into the bathroom in the dark, and Rikki could see his eyes glitter.

'Now, if I kill him here, Nagaina will know; and if I fight him on the open floor, the odds are in his favour. What am I to do?' said Rikki-tikki-tavi.

Nag waved to and fro, and then Rikki-tikki heard him drinking from the biggest water-jar that was used to fill the bath. 'That is good,' said the snake. 'Now, when Karait was killed, the big man had a stick. He may have that stick still, but when he comes in to bathe in the morning he will not have a stick. I shall wait here till he comes. Nagaina—do you hear me?—I shall wait here in the cool till daytime.'

There was no answer from outside, so Rikki-tikki knew Nagaina had gone away. Nag coiled himself down, coil by coil, round the bulge at the bottom of the water-jar, and Rikki-tikki stayed still as death. After an hour he began to move, muscle by muscle, toward the jar. Nag was asleep, and Rikki-tikki looked at his big back, wondering which would be the best place for a good hold. 'If I don't break his back at the first jump,' said Rikki-tikki, 'he can still fight; and if he fights—O Rikki!' He looked at the thickness of the neck below the hood, but that was too much for him; and a bite near the tail would only make Nag savage.

'It must be the head,' he said at last; 'the head above the hood; and, when I am once there, I must not let go.'

Then he jumped. The head was lying a little clear of the water-jar, under the curve of it; and, as his teeth met, Rikki braced his back against the bulge of the red earthenware to hold down the head. This gave him just one second's purchase, and he made the most of it. Then he was battered to and fro as a rat is shaken by a dog—to and fro on the floor, up and down, and round in great circles; but his eyes were red, and he held on as the body cartwhipped over the floor, upsetting the tin dipper and the soap-dish and the flesh-brush, and banged against the tin side of the bath. As he held he closed his jaws tighter, and tighter, for he felt sure he would be banged to death, and, for the honour of his family, he preferred to be found with his teeth locked. He was dizzy, aching, and felt shaken to pieces when something went off like a thunderclap just behind him; a hot wind knocked him senseless and red fire singed his fur. The big man had been wakened by the noise, and had fired both barrels of a shot-gun into Nag just behind the hood.

Rikki-tikki held on with his eyes shut, for now he was quite sure he was dead; but the head did not move, and the big man picked him up and said, 'It's the mongoose again,

Alice; the little chap has saved our lives now.'

Then Teddy's mother came in with a very white face, and saw what was left of Nag, and Rikki-tikki dragged himself to Teddy's bedroom and spent half the rest of the night shaking himself tenderly to find out whether he really was broken into forty pieces, as he fancied.

When morning came he was very stif, but well pleased with his doings. 'Now I have Nagaina to settle with, and she will be worse than five Nags, and there's no knowing when the eggs she spoke of will hatch. Goodness! I must go and see Darzee,' he said.

Without waiting for breakfast, Rikki-tikki ran to the thornbush where Darzee was singing a song of triumph at the top of his voice. The news of Nag's death was all over the garden, for the sweeper had thrown the body on the rubbish-heap.

'Oh, you stupid tuft of feathers!' said Rikki-tikki, angrily. 'Is this the time to sing?'

'Nag is dead—is dead—is dead!' sang Darzee. 'The valiant Rikki-tikki caught him by the head and held fast. The big man brought the bang-stick and Nag fell in two pieces! He will never eat my babies again.'

'All that's true enough; but where's Nagaina?' said Rikki-tikki, looking carefully round him.

'Nagaina came to the bathroom sluice and called for Nag,' Darzee went on; 'and Nag came out on the end of a stick— the sweeper picked him up on the end of a stick and threw him upon the rubbish-heap. Let us sing about the great, the red-eyed Rikki-tikki!' and Darzee filled his throat and sang.

'If I could get up to your nest, I'd roll all your babies out!' said Rikki-tikki. 'You don't know when to do the right thing at the right time. You're safe enough in your nest there, but it's war for me down here. Stop singing a minute, Darzee.'

'For the great, the beautiful Rikki-tikki's sake I will stop,' said Darzee. 'What is it, O killer of the terrible Nag!'

'Where is Nagaina, for the third time?'

'On the rubbish-heap by the stables, mourning for Nag. Great is Rikki-tikki with the white teeth.'

'Bother my white teeth! Have you ever heard where she keeps her eggs?'

'In the melon-bed, on the end nearest the wall, where the sun strikes nearly all day. She had them there weeks ago.'

'And you never thought it worth while to tell me? The end nearest the wall, you said?'

'Rikki-tikki, you are not going to eat her eggs?'

Not eat exactly; no. Darzee, if you have a grain of sense you will fly off to the stables and pretend that your wing is broken, and let Nagaina chase you away to this bush. I must get to the melon-bed, and if I went there now she'd see me.'

Darzee was a feather-brained little fellow who could never hold more than one idea at a time in his head and just because he knew that Nagaina's children were born in eggs like his own, he didn't think at first that it was fair to kill them. But his wife was a sensible bird, and she knew that cobra's eggs meant young cobras later on; so she flew off from the nest, and left Darzee to keep the babies warm, and continue his song about the death of Nag. Darzee was very like a man in some ways.

She fluttered in front of Nagaina by the rubbish-heap, and cried out, 'Oh, my wing is broken! The boy in the house threw a stone at me and broke it.' Then she fluttered more desperately than ever.

Nagaina lifted up her head and hissed, 'You warned Rikki-tikki when I would have killed him. Indeed and truly, you've chosen a bad place to be lame in.' And she moved toward Darzee's wife, slipping along over the dust. 'The boy broke it with a stone!' shrieked Darzee's wife.

'Well! It may be some consolation to you when you're dead to know that I shall settle accounts with the boy. My husband lies on the rubbish-heap this morning, but before night the boy in the house will lie very still. What is the use of running away? I am sure to catch you. Little fool, look at me!'

Darzee's wife knew better than to do *that,* for a bird who looks at a snake's eyes gets so frightened that she cannot move. Darzee's wife fluttered on, piping sorrowfully, and never leaving the ground, and Nagaina quickened her pace.

Rikki-tikki heard them going up the path from the stables, and he raced for the end of the melon-patch near the wall. There, in the warm litter about the melons, very cunningly hidden, he found twenty-five eggs, about the size of a bantam's eggs, but with whitish skin instead of shell.

'I was not a day too soon,' he said; for he could see the baby cobras curled up inside the skin, and he knew that the minute they were hatched they could each kill a man or a mongoose. He bit off the tops of the eggs as fast as he could, taking care to crush the young cobras, and turned over the litter from time to time to see whether he had missed any. At last there were only three eggs left, and Rikki-tikki began to chuckle to himself, when he heard Darzee's wife screaming, 'Rikki-tikki, I led Nagaina toward the house, and she has gone into the veranda, and—oh, come quickly she means killing.'

Rikki-tikki smashed two eggs, and tumbled backward down the melon-bed with the third egg in his mouth, and scuttled to the veranda as hard as he could put foot to the ground. Teddy and his mother and father were there at early breakfast; but Rikki-tikki saw that they were not eating anything. They sat stone-still, and their faces were white. Nagaina was coiled up on the matting by Teddy's chair, within easy striking distance of Teddy's bare leg, and she was swaying to and fro singing a song of triumph.

'Son of the big man that killed Nag,' she hissed, 'stay still. I am not ready yet. Wait a little. Keep very still, all you three. If you move I strike, and if you do not move I strike. Oh, foolish people, who killed my Nag!'

Teddy's eyes were fixed on his father, and all his father could do was to whisper, 'Sit still, Teddy. You mustn't move. Teddy, keep still.'

Then Rikki-tikki came up and cried, 'Turn round, Nagaina; turn and fight!'

'All in good time,' said she, without moving her eyes. 'I will settle my account with you presently. Look at your friends, Rikki-tikki. They are still and white; they are afraid. They dare not move, and if you come a step nearer I strike.'

'Look at your eggs,' said Rikki-tikki, 'in the melon-bed near the wall. Go and look, Nagaina.'

The big snake turned half round, and saw the egg on the veranda. 'Ah-h! Give it to me,' she said.

Rikki-tikki put his paws one on each side of the egg, and his eyes were blood-red. 'What price for a snake's egg? For a young cobra? For a young king-cobra? For the last—the very last of the brood? The ants are eating all the others down by the melon-bed.'

Nagaina spun clear round, forgetting everything for the sake of the one egg; and Rikki-tikki saw Teddy's father shoot out a big hand, catch Teddy by the shoulder, and drag him across the little table with the tea-cups, safe and out of reach of Nagaina.

'Tricked! Tricked! Tricked! Rikk-tck-tck!' chuckled Rikki-tikki. 'The boy is safe, and it was I—I—I that caught Nag by the hood last night in the bathroom.' Then he began to jump up and down, all four feet together, his head close to the floor. 'He threw me to and fro, but he could not shake me off. He was dead before the big man blew him in two. I did it. Rikki-tikki-tck-tck! Come then, Nagaina. Come and fight with me. You shall not be a widow long.'

Nagaina saw that she had lost her chance of killing Teddy, and the egg lay between Rikki-tikki's paws. 'Give me the egg, Rikki-tikki. Give me the last of my eggs, and I will go away and never come back,' she said, lowering her hood.

'Yes, you will go away, and you will never come back; for you will go to the rubbish-heap with Nag. Fight, widow! The big man has gone for his gun! Fight!'

Rikki-tikki was bounding all round Nagaina, keeping just out of reach of her stroke, his little eyes like hot coals. Nagaina gathered herself together, and flung out at him. Rikki-tikki jumped up and backward. Again and again and again she struck, and each time her head came with a whack on the matting of the veranda and she gathered herself together like a watch-spring. Then Rikki-tikki danced in a circle to get behind her, and Nagaina spun round to keep her head to his head, so that the rustle of her tail on the matting sounded like dry leaves blown along by the wind.

He had forgotten the egg. It still lay on the veranda, and Nagaina came nearer and nearer to it, till at last, while Rikki-tikki was drawing breath, she caught it in her mouth, turned to the veranda steps, and flew like an arrow down the path, with Rikki-tikki behind her. When the cobra runs for her life, she goes like a whiplash flicked across a horse's neck.

Rikki-tikki knew that he must catch, her, or all the trouble would begin again. She headed straight for the long grass by the thorn-bush, and as he was running Rikki-tikki heard Darzee still singing his foolish little song of triumph. But Darzee's wife was wiser. She flew off her nest as Nagaina came along, and flapped her wings about Nagaina's head. If Darzee had helped they might have turned her; but Nagaina only lowered her hood and went on. Still, the instant's delay brought Rikki-tikki up to her, and as she plunged into the rat-hole where she and Nag used to live, his little white teeth were clenched on her tail, and he went down with her—and very few mongooses, however wise and old they may be, care to follow a cobra into its hole. It was dark in the hole; and Rikki-tikki *never* knew when it might open out and give Nagaina room to turn and strike at him. He held on savagely, and struck out his feet to act as brakes on the dark slope of the hot, moist earth.

Then the grass by the mouth of the hole stopped waving, and Darzee said, 'It is all over with Rikki-tikki! We must sing his death-song. Valiant Rikki-tikki is dead! For Nagaina will surely kill him underground.' So he sang a very mournful song that he made up all on the spur of the minute, and just as he got to the most touching part the grass quivered again, and Rikki-tikki, covered with dirt, dragged himself out of the hole leg by leg, licking his whiskers. Darzee stopped with a little shout. Rikki-tikki shook some of the dust out of his fur and sneezed.

'It is all over,' he said. 'The widow will never come out again.' And the red ants that live between the grass stems heard him, and began to troop down one after another to see if he had spoken the truth.

Rikki-tikki curled himself up in the grass and slept where he was—slept and slept till it was late in the afternoon, for he had done a hard day's work.

'Now,' he said, when he awoke, 'I will go back to the house. Tell the Coppersmith, Darzee, and he will tell the garden that Nagaina is dead.'

The Coppersmith is a bird who makes a noise exactly like the beating of a little hammer on a copper pot; and the reason he is always making it is because he is the town-crier to every Indian garden, and tells all the news to everybody who cares to listen. As Rikki-tikki went up the path, he heard his 'attention' notes like a tiny dinner-gong; and then the steady *'Ding-dong-tock! Nag is dead—dong! Nagaina is dead! Ding-dong—tock!'* That set all the birds in the garden singing, and the frogs croaking; for Nag and Nagaina used to eat frogs as well as little birds.

When Rikki got to the house, Teddy and Teddy's mother (she looked very white still, for she had been fainting) and Teddy's father came out and almost cried over him; and that night he ate all that was given him till he could eat no more, and went to bed on Teddy's shoulder, where Teddy's mother saw him when she came to look late at night.

'He saved our lives and Teddy's life,' she said to her husband. 'Just think, he saved all our lives.'

Rikki-tikki woke up with a jump, for all mongooses are light sleepers.

'Oh, it's you,' said he. 'What are you bothering for? All the cobras are dead; and if they weren't, I'm here.'

Rikki-tikki had a right to be proud of himself; but he did not grow too proud, and he kept that garden as a mongoose should keep it, with tooth and jump and spring and bite, till never a cobra dared show its head inside the walls.

DARZEE'S CHANT
(Sung in Honour of Rikki-tikki-tavi)

Singer and tailor am I—
Doubled the joys that I know

Proud of my lilt through the sky,
Proud of the house that I saw—
Over and under, so weave I my music—so weave I the
house that I sew.
Sing to your fledglings again,
Mother, oh lift up your head!
Evil that plagued us is slain,
Death in the garden lies dead.
Terror that hid in the roses is important—flung on the
dung-hill and dead
Who hath delivered us, who?
Tell me his nest and his name.
Rikki, the valiant, the true,
Tikki, with eyeballs of flame.
Rik-tikki-tikki, the ivory fanged, the hunter with eyeballs
of flame.
Give him the Thanks of the Birds,
Bowing with tail feathers spread)
Praise him with nightingale words—
Nay, I will praise him instead.
Heart! I will sing you the praise of the bottle-tailed
Rikki, with eyeballs of red,

(Here Rikki-tikki interrupted, and the rest of the song is lost.)

THE HAUNTS OF ISABELINE

C.H. Donald

I

It has been a severe winter in the Himalayas, and an early one, but once more the sun shines bright and warm, and green patches of grass here and there, in a great wilderness of dazzling white snow, acknowledge its power and the advent of spring. A flock of light-hearted little choughs circling in the bright blue sky above sing to each other, and convey the joyful tidings to all whom they may concern, that the snow is fast melting from their feeding grounds, and that it is high time to be out and enjoying life in such glorious weather.

Isabeline, the little brown mother bear, hears the call, and pokes her nose out of her hollow at the root of an ancient mountain oak, where she has spent the winter, and given birth to two tiny wee cubs. The nose is followed by a great shaggy head and two little beads of eyes, blinking hard in the glare, roll in their sockets, while her nose wobbles about from side to side, to ascertain from every passing zephyr of the presence of any lurking enemy. Her keen scent, however, tells her that all is well, and that she may leave her two woolly balls and come out. Stealthily a great paw, armed with large white nails, next makes an appearance, and then the whole bear in all her glory of a magnificent winter coat, steps out into the sun, to stretch her weary limbs after her long winter sleep. She can still hear the cry of the choughs far, far above her, as she looks up the valley to the alpine pastures which she knows so well, and slowly she moves off in that direction, her legs so stiff that they have some difficulty in bearing her weight, but at each step they get better, and soon 'Isabeline' is well above the forests and resettling in the warm sun.

There is, however, no time for enjoyment and the pangs of hunger must be first attended to, before she hurries back to the little ones in the cave. The sight that meets her eyes on everyside is not very reassuring and there does not seem very much prospect of satisfying her ravenous appetite on these snow-covered slopes, but she sees the little green path and makes for it and is rewarded for her pains by getting a few mouthfulls of luscious young, wild carrot tops, as *hors d'oeuvre*. Thence she slowly makes her way down again, turning over all the big stones she passes and getting from under one, a nest of beetles or ant's larvae, and under the next a few blades of sprouting grasses, till eventually she finds herself in a ravine, from the side of which all the snow has been blown off by the wind and the grass coming up sweet and green everywhere, and here she makes up for lost time. As she feeds on she becomes aware that she is not the first of her kind that has visited this spot during that morning, and her nose tells her that another has gone over the same ground, only a few hours before her, but there is no time to think of others, as she goes from tuft to tuft, and here and there turns over a stone to see if it conceals anything edible, beneath it.

She is not nearly satisfied, but the sun is high up in the horizon, and it's time that she made her way back to the little ones at home, as it is not safe to wander about at a time when her arch enemy, man, may be about. Day after day she might be seen grazing on the bare plateaux, in the early mornings, and late evenings, and as the snow melts, new pastures come into being, and she has much less difficulty in satisfying her cravings than she formerly had.

Spring has past into summer, and the snow has given place to green fields of grass and flowers of every hue. Masses of dainty primulae, king-cups and anenomes, clothe the plateaux on every side in gay pinks, yellows and purples, whilst a bright patch of blue tells of a bed of little forget-me-nots or gentians, and there on that crag, all by itself, too proud to mix with the rest, waves gently in the breeze, the gem of the mountains, in its wonderful electric blue, the blue mountain poppy.

The little cubs have been all over these hills with their mother, since we last saw her, and though only three months old now, are fine sturdy little specimens, and up to every kind of mischief their ursine brains can devise. In size there is practically no difference between them, and in colour they are identical, except that the one has a small white waistcoat which is almost indistinguishable in the other. In temperament however, they are as the poles apart, and if you could only get near enough to see the wee, restive little beady eyes of each, you could have no doubt as to which had the wits of the family.

I had seen old 'Isabeline' on the very first occasion that she had ventured out of her hollow in the tree, and I had from afar, coveted that glossy, light brown winter coat of hers, which I had examined carefully through my glasses, and as she approached the green patch in the snow, she little guessed, poor little lady, how near she was to feeling a rifle bullet smashing through her bones. I, too, had seen the green patch and knew she would go to it, so keeping the spur of the hill between us, had reached a point a few yards above it, just before her, and watched her as she grazed. I had seen that beautiful coat, but I had also seen something else, when she came to within 30 yards of me, which the glasses had not revealed, and which proved her salvation.

This was the lack of hair, in patches, underneath, which showed me that she was the mother of one, if not two little babies which eagerly waited for her arrival, and would starve in their cave if some cruel hand laid her low now. From that date on she became my especial care, and many and many is the time, that I have sat and watched her turning over the boulders and grazing on the grassy slopes, little dreaming how near she was to her enemy, who, for the time being, was also her friend. When 'Devil' and 'Fool', as I christened the cubs, first made their appearance in public, early in June, I had the good fortune to meet them at very close quarters, without their knowing it, and from that hour fell in love with them, and was determined to have them for my own, but how to get them, without shooting the mother, was another matter altogether. However, there was no hurry and I could afford to wait and watch, and before long got to recognize the one from the other almost as well as the mother could have done. There was something in the Devil's eyes and general saucy devil-may-care look that was quite wanting in poor Fool. It was not only in his eyes but in his general demeanour, for it was not necessary to be near him to be able to recognize him, he was unmistakable 40 yards away.

What it was, I could not tell, but it was there, and if anyone who had never seen the cubs before, had been asked which was Devil and which Fool he would have pointed them out

The Haunts of Isabeline ▪ 33

correctly, the very first shot.

One evening I had gone up for a quiet stroll to Isabeline's haunts; it was a warm afternoon and very still, even at this altitude, and whilst waiting under a rock, I had got drowsy and fallen asleep.

I woke up with a start hearing strange noises somewhere very near, and there to my delight, not ten yards away, embracing each other, were Devil and Fool. Such a time as they were having, on the soft turf, and the mother a few yards below, not taking the least notice of her dear little hopefuls' gambol. This was luck, the wind blew directly from them to me, so there was no possibility of my being winded, and until it changed, or they got above me, I would be able to feast my eyes on their delightful antics. The fond embrace in which I first saw them, culminated in the Fool losing his balance and toppling over with the Devil still holding on to him, and down they went rolling in a ball for a few yards, when Devil loosened his hold, and ran for his mother. Right under her legs he rushed, and then turning round, stood up on his hind legs, with his forepaws on her back, and coyly peeped at Fool from this coign of vantage. I just suppressed a loud laugh, for anything more grotesque than the Devil's rolling eyes and twitching snout, and the poor Fool's tired look and perplexity, would be hard to find. After a couple of seconds or so, Fool too made a rush for his mother's legs, evidently hoping to get a grip of Devil from below, but Devil had played this game before, seemingly, and was prepared, for as soon as Fool emerged on the other side, Devil fell on his back, with both paws firmly gripping Fool's sides and his teeth in Fool's neck, and thus got quite a pleasant little-ride at, Fool's expense, till his weight brought Fool down on his nose. Up got Devil again, and made for his mother, and Fool, picking himself up, quietly set about following his mother's example and feeding. The Devil, though, was irrepressible, and, not finding Fool sociably inclined, he looked at his mother as much as to say 'shall I?' and began tearing up the ground with his forefeet, and backing at the same time, then suddenly made a plunge at her, but evidently rather misjudged his distance, for he landed right on her head, which had the effect of jabbing her snout rather violently into the ground. Next instant old Devil was flying through space as though out of a gun barrel, and landed on his back quite ten feet down the hill. The mother went on with her grazing and took no further interest but the Devil's face was a treat. He stood up and looked at his mother out of the corner of his eye, and such a look!

I am sure that had he been able to speak English, the words he would have muttered would have been 'nasty old cat'. He could not have expressed himself more plainly than he did, though.

Now this would probably have kept Devil quiet for some time, and made him think of more serious things, but just then he looked up and his eye met Fool's, in which he plainly saw written the words 'that served you jolly well right', and that coming from Fool was not to be endured at any price, so he made a savage charge at him, and once again I saw them in a loving embrace, but this time they had both got a good deal to say to each other as they rolled down, locked in each other's arms, and from the way it was all said, I knew it was nasty names that they were calling each other. A depression in the ground hid them from my view for a few seconds, and what was my surprise to suddenly hear the angry 'unf unf unf' half sneeze, half grunt of a bear alarmed, and angry. Up went the mother's head in a second, with her nose held well to the wind, and giving vent to a deeper 'unf unf unf' than the last I had heard, off she went, after Devil and Fool, but pulled up at the top of the depression, where I could still see her, with all the long hair on her whiskers bristling with anger, at something I could not see. The babies had both now joined their mother and all three stood looking down at, to me, the unknown disturber of their peace.

What could it be? Not a man, for they would not stand there looking at him, and besides, there were no shepherds on this plateau as yet, and nobody but a shepherd would come here. I began to get as excited as the bears were, but could not move from my rock without attracting the attention of one or the other of the three before me, so had to curb my impatience and sit where I was, but was soon rewarded, for the mother gradually edged off and down into the depression and both the cubs followed. I was out of my hiding at once, and taking advantage of a small spur behind one got quickly round it.

As my head got over the rising ground, the breeze brought up the shrill 'chick chick' constantly repeated notes of the monaul pheasant, this also was his note of alarm and warning, but far down in the valley.

With my glasses I searched every inch of the rolling plateaux before me and below me, but not a thing could I see anywhere, and yet I felt certain that something was astir somewhere, what could it be?

Just as I was getting tired of looking at nothing, a movement a long way down the hill caught my eye, but look as I would nothing could I make of it, though I gazed again and again with a powerful pair of Zeiss glasses, at the exact spot where I had seen the movement with the naked eye. Looking still lower down, I suddenly spotted a fox digging for voles some 200 yards below where I had first seen the 'movement'.

This would account for the cry of alarm of the monaul, but did not in the least explain the uneasiness of the bears, or that 'movement' I saw. Still worried, I kept on looking at the fox, a tiny speck in the distance, when again that movement caught my eye, and much more distinct this time. Again I got the glasses out and looked and looked till my eyes ached, but nothing was visible, and yet I was sure that I was not mistaken. More puzzled than ever, I decided to watch the country around the fox for a few minutes, and before a couple of minutes had gone I distinctly saw a greyish object flash through the air and again disappear into the very bowels of the earth. Again my glasses revealed nothing, for some time, but at length, on a grey boulder, I noticed the twitch of a tail, and there right before me, was a beautiful panther crouching low on the rock. I must have had my eyes and glasses on him over and over again, and yet not seen him, and now that I had seen him, he was as plain almost as the bears had been a few minutes previously. It was absurd to risk a 400 yards long shot, but how was I to get nearer in such open country, was the question? But then again why those sudden movements on his part and why was he now crouching on that rock?

Then a thought struck me. He was stalking the fox. If so, that would be something worth watching, and I soon forgot all about Isabeline and her family and settled myself to watch developments in this direction. For five full minutes that panther sat immovable as the rock on which he crouched, and then without a moment's warning or the slightest movement of a muscle, he sprang straight into the air and stopped dead on a rock some ten feet lower down, in the identical position in which he left the last rock. I looked at the fox but she had noticed nothing, and was moving leisurely about in quest of her voles. The next move of the panther was different, and he sprang lightly off the rock and crouching low, went very stealthily yet with quick steps, down the hill. This time the fox looked up, and immediately the panther crouched and lay still. The fox, however, like me, had got a glimpse of something and though not scared, was still suspicious and kept looking up every few seconds, but the panther never moved a muscle, and only about 80 to 100 yards divided them.

Gazing through binoculars for any length of time is very tiring for the eyes, and though loth to miss a single state of the drama before me, I put them down till the feline should again make a move, keeping my eyes on him in the meantime. It was about 10 minutes ere he moved again and this time covered a good 20 paces ere he stopped, but the fox too was changing her ground and still kept her distance. She was now no longer straight below him as she had been when I first saw him, but had got several yards to one side, yet he still went on straight down.

Could he have lost sight of her, and is he making for the place he last saw her in, from the rock, in the fond hope that she is still there? Not much fear of his taking those all-seeing eyes of his off her for a single second. I soon saw his little game; there was a huge rock some 30 feet to the rear of the fox and he meant to get that between him and her as soon as possible. A slight pause of a few seconds and as the fox did not look up, he moved stealthily forward and got on to a rock and very slowly peered over. The little fox still merrily went from hole to hole, noising each, oblivious of all danger, and as she turned her back for a second, I saw a sight I shall never forget.

The panther had been looking over the rock at the time, with his fore paws resting on it and his hind feet on the ground below, and yet from that non-jumping attitude, he sprang clear 20 feet or so down, and looked for all the world like a shooting star. This spring and a rush and he was behind the coveted rock, but what in the meantime had alarmed the fox? She was not looking in his direction, but rather down the hill and below him, yet 'pheaw pheaw-aw-aw' came her long warning cry.

I could no longer see the panther now, but knew he was only waiting for the fox to turn her head, and she was as good as dead, and then, perhaps I might have a chance of a stalk after him. The fox looks this way and that, undoubtedly alarmed, but unaware of the cause of it. Some wonderful instinct warning her to be on her guard, for what else could it be that alarmed her? Had it been some sound the feline made, or had she got his scent, she would have run off some distance away from either, before turning to 'pheaw' but it is something in no way located, yet she is aware in some vague way of the presence of danger.

It comes too; as she turns her head there is a mighty rush, and a something with the speed of a falcon is on her, almost before she has time to look back, but there again, that something has befriended her, and with a sudden whisk of her tail, and a twist that my eye could not even follow, she has evaded those relentless talons, and somehow doubled under the panther's legs and is flying for life down the hill, to find cover in the birch jungle below. Strangely enough the panther never even attempted to follow, but accepted his defeat, and sat down on a rock and watched the fox racing down the hill. I could hear the 'pheaws' coming up from the forest below, for a long time after.

I carefully changed my position and getting into a dip of the hill crawled round till I got a ridge in between myself and the feline, and then ran as hard as I could for a spot I marked out in my mind as being within 100 yards of him, and arriving there, stalked very carefully over, till I could get my eyes just over the top, but he was 'non est'.

High and low I searched, but not a sign of him could I find and as night was fast approaching, I had to make my way back to camp, and leave him.

II

In the meantime, while I interested myself in the panther and his doings, Isabeline and her cubs had wandered out of sight, and I saw them no more for some time to come. I had rather wondered at the bears giving their note of alarm for a panther, and I do not suppose that a solitary one would have bothered his head much about him one way or the other, but with a mother with tiny cubs, it is different, as Mr Spots would not hesitate long about making a meal off a cub if he got the chance, and Isabeline had long ago taught Devil and Food to be careful of his scent, and warn her at once should they come across it.

I have already said that I had wanted to capture the cubs and have them as pets, but one cannot go and shoot an animal one has taken an interest in for over a month, in cold blood, though I have no doubt, had I seen her with the cubs the first time she came out, I should not have thought twice about it. The next time I came across them, the summer had given place to late autumn, the sheep had left the alpine pastures, the flowers had bowed their heads to the cutting winds, and the glorious verdant carpets on which Devil and Fool had been wont to play had assumed a sombre brown. In the valley below, the birch and maples had clothed themselves in their golden tints, and lower still could be seen the brilliant scarlet of the virginian creeper clustering about the dark green of the spruce and silver-fir.

The scene in all its wonderful variety of colours, even though it lacked the vivid greens of spring, defied description. Above, the grand old giants reared their virgin snow-capped peaks into the clear blue sky, and in the gorge, just below that mighty peak, a glacier grim, glistened with blues and greens as the rays of the morning sun touched it.

Well might Isabeline be proud of her lovely haunts, and loth to leave them till the bleak winter winds and hard frosts which made digging impossible, drove her down to more sheltered nooks. The hardy 'bhurrel', the blue sheep of the Himalayas can alone face those icy blasts, and appears to revel in the blizzards that howl round his inhospitable, rugged peaks.

As soon as the frost sets in, and even Isabeline's great claws and forearm can make no impression on the hard ground, she thinks of looking about for a sequestered home in which to spend the winter. A cave beneath an overhanging rock, or the hollow at the root of a tree, which will keep her warm and dry and yet permit the passage of fresh air, are selected with much care, for her long winter sleep. She will enter it a fat tubby ball, almost round, and issue four to five months later, simply skin and bone, but the possessor of a lovely coat.

It was in late October, when I came across Isabeline and her cubs. The latter were now well grown, and to catch them would have been no easy matter, so I was obliged to give up all thought of it, but my interest in them had not abated in the slightest and I was as ready as ever to watch them at their play. Determined to find out their hibernating quarters, I used to be up on their feeding grounds before the sun touched them and on the first occasion contented myself by watching them leave for the trees, as the day advanced, through my glasses. But that proved a fruitless watch, as I lost sight of them as soon as they got into the forest.

The next time, some ten days later, I decided to follow them, but the ground being caked and hard with frost, I had the greatest difficulty in seeing their tracks, and lost them entirely in the forest, where they went over a succession of rocks and boulders. The following week a light fall of snow came to my help, and the morning after it, I made my way up to her favourite ravine and was just in time to see her and the cubs disappearing into some birch jungle. There was no mistaking their tracks now, and on hands and knees I crawled after them among the dense tangle of branches which being bent down year after year by the winter snows, grow down instead of standing up straight.

Careful not to get too near or disturb them in any way, I carefully avoided each branch, either stepping over or crawling under it. Thus I must have covered over a mile, and was thankful to find myself getting into more open cover, the birch giving place to oak and pine. All this time I had not got a single glimpse of them, though I know from the tracks that I was very near. Under one tree I found marks of the mother's claws, where she had raked up some twigs and branches, preparatory to lying down for the day, but had changed her mind and moved on. This at all events meant that she would not go very much further and it behoved me to be all the more careful, in case I stumbled on to her unawares from below, in which case she might charge and tend to make things nasty, in defence of her cubs.

I had my trusty rifle with me, but there are times when it is difficult to be quick enough with it, and this might be one of them. Carefully, with one eye on the tracks and the other on the ground ahead, I plodded on, removing every twig that chanced in my way, and to my joy I at last came to where the tracks began moving downhill. This gave me a much better command of the position and also enabled me to see further. A bear, brown or black, if he selects a tree to sit behind, will almost invariably sit on the upper side and not below it, so I should now have a chance of seeing the family from some distance if they meant to sleep under a tree and not go into a cave, which at this season, however, was unlikely.

On the other hand, this would not help me to find, their hibernating quarters, but having come so far, I intended to continue now, wherever they went, and follow them. A tragopan gave me the first intimation of their exact whereabouts, for not 50 yards ahead, I could hear his plaintive cry as, disturbed by their approach, he rushed up the hill uttering his curious single note. This meant that I could hurry on for a few paces, as a spur divided us, and any noise I made would not reach them, but I must be careful not to frighten the tragopan unduly and make him fly, as that might put the bears on the *qui vive*.

The bears had not wasted their time while seeking their place for the midday siesta, as over-turned stones and logs of wood testified, and in one place I had to make a dive into some undergrowth to avoid a nest of angry jungle wasps, whose home had been ruthlessly torn out and their winter store of honey robbed by the furry marauders ahead.

A musk-deer near whose lair they passed, stood up and gave his cry of alarm—'fitch fitch'—at intervals of a few seconds, and so engaged was he in looking at the bears, that I got to within 30 feet of him, and could see his gleaming white tushes and saw him stamp his foot, as he 'fitched' and wagged his little scut.

One ear was held forward and the other twitching back and fro, alive to every sound. I crouched behind a stump and very gently 'fitched' in return. In a second his head turned in my direction, and he stood staring intently, not being able to make it out, the very embodiment of grace and daintiness. I dare not alarm him or he might go racing off down the hill in his succession of jumps, a mode of locomotion, peculiar to the little beasts, and yet I must get him away from here, before I could move myself, and in the meantime, the bears were getting further and further away. 'Fitch fitch' I said to him and 'fitch sh sh' was his reply, and a violent stamp on the ground. A second 'fitch' from me was too much for his nerves and had the desired effect. With half a dozen dainty little bounds, all four legs rising and falling at the same time, he fled up the hill and with a final 'fitch' disappeared from view behind some rocks.

Again I moved forward and, climbing a small rise over which the tracks led me, looked down on an expanse of melting snow and at the foot of it saw Devil and Fool playing hide and seek. Glancing at the tracks, I could see that they had not troubled to walk down, but had simply glissaded or rolled the whole way to the bottom. Even Isabeline had become playful after her slide, for, as one of the cubs ran round her, she got up on her hind legs, her great fat forearms swaying from side to side, and gave vent to a loud snort ending up with a tremendous puff as though blowing bubbles.

Little Fool rushed up and also got on to his hind legs in front of her, and the pair promptly set to work to do a little boxing, but Devil did not see why he should be left out in the cold, and made for poor Fool. A fair spar, with the mother as umpire, ensued, but as usual it did not last long and ended up in close grips and a roll in the snow. Devil's honour was satisfied and once more the trio started off up the opposite hill, and I had to sit where I was till they went round the next spur, and once more took up the trail from the next ridge.

I had been most fortunate all this time in having the wind blowing down hill, but it was now time for it to change. In the Himalayas the wind usually blows down the valleys from 4 or 5 o'clock in the afternoon till 8 or 9 a.m. the following morning, and uphill for the rest of the day, but this fact would not trouble me so long as the bears kept to the contour of the hills, but if they suddenly went down a valley I should be discovered at once if I attempted to follow, so in that case I would have to wait till they had climbed up the other side.

As I topped the crest I found before me a ravine covered with a forest of spruce and silver-fir, and now left convinced that this was the place the bears had been making for, and would now lie up under some old forest giant. Nor was I wrong. Just below me was the tree they had selected for their seista the previous day, but now they had gone down lower, and I must be cautious as they might come to a halt any moment. I crawled along a few paces and was pulled up short by hearing a twig crack, and peeping round the trunk of a tree, I espied Isabeline busy making up a snug bed for herself, and both the cubs interestedly watching operations.

Foiled in my hopes of seeing their winter quarters I took my sandwiches out of my pocket and proceeded to replenish the inner man, and at the same time keep an eye on the bears. Having removed any stones or hard twigs from under her, the old lady sat up on her haunches and had a good look all round, with her nose well to the wind. Satisfied that all was well she thought about attending to her toilet. A great big hind paw began very deliberately scratching the back of her head and, that done, she lay down with both her fore-paws in front of her and surveyed her huge white claws. Devil still had something on his mind and went down a little way to investigate the roots of another tree, but Fool sat down alongside his mother and getting his hind foot into his mouth, was busy for the next ten minutes sucking it, making an extraordinary gurgling the while. Devil too came up and joined the other two, and half an hour from the time they arrived there everyone was sound asleep, bunched close together. Even though I had seen them settle themselves, I could not make out where one began or the other ended. They looked like one great brown stone except for the fact that every now and again a puff of wind stirred the hair on one of their backs. There was nothing now left for me to do, but to get back home, but before doing so, I would give them a chance of winding me, to see if they kept their noses open even in sleep.

Going back over the spur I had just come over, I descended to their level and quietly got some 20 yards below their tree and hid myself behind another. I had not been there many seconds, when a small head looked round the edge, the nose well in the air and working vigorously, and with a low 'unf unf unf' awoke the other two. Both the cubs took to their heels up the hill but the mother waited just long enough to see that nothing followed, and then went after her sons. Their education had not been neglected, evidently, and the mother no doubt was not a little proud of her apt pupils. Had I not seen them go off I might have passed them within a few yards and never known that there was a bear within a mile of me, so quietly had they all disappeared. Fortunately for mother bear, in the Higher Himalayas there is so very little that can harm her or her young that she can instruct them pretty thoroughly as to what they should avoid.

'All man's scents are not necessarily dangerous but it is as well to steer clear of them all. That which is tainted with the smell of goat and sheep, or with that of cows and buffaloes, you need not run from, but just get out of his way and get behind a log or a tree till he has passed. If it is pure man's scent, whether he means mischief or not, fly the moment you get it, and keep to thick scrub as long as you can till well out of his reach, and then go over all the stones and rocks you can find to leave no track. If you get the smell of a panther, give me warning, and keep near me. Goats and sheep are very nice eating but do not go too near a flock while it is still light, unless you can find a straggler. Beware of a flock with which there is smell of dog, as they will bark and rouse the camp and guide the men on your scent, and you will have to give up your dinner even if you have had the luck to get it away. You will be a match for any two or three dogs, but you can do nothing when the dogs are followed by half a dozen men armed with big sticks. Buffaloes will do you no harm if you do them none, and though our cousin the black bear has no difficulty in killing them now and again, and we are stronger than he, yet he has got sharp claws with which he can get a firm hold on the back of a buffalo and so hang on till the animal becomes frantic, and falls over a cliff or breaks a leg, but our claws are no good for that sort of thing, being meant only for digging. The same applies to cows and bullocks, though when you are full grown you may be able to manage a cow, but be careful, as sometimes one or two of the bulls with the herd may charge, and in the open, he will get the best of it. A wheat crop is a very pleasant place to spend a night in, but if grazing is good in our own haunts eschew such luxuries, as they are often fraught with danger, and if it is known that we make raids on the crops, a man with a gun may be there in hiding to receive you one night. Keep to your own lovely feeding grounds, and follow the instructions I have so often drummed into your heads and you will live to be as old as you desire, but remember that curiosity killed the cat, and will be the end of you, if you are not very careful.'

The advice was good, and though curiosity was Devil's besetting sin, he was getting over it as he grew up, and after the one or two frights his mother gave him, began to learn that it was enough for him to discover the presence of danger through his nose, without trying to see it as well.

Eighteen months went by, and I had not been able to visit the haunts of Isabeline again, but I had heard of her and the cubs, now grown almost as big as herself, from shepherds and others who had spent the preceding summer near her. Three bears always together, had been frequently reported to me, but no one had ever feared of them attacking sheep, but of late, one huge beast had also taken up his quarters and he had done a good deal of damage among the flocks.

The villagers had begged me to go up and shoot him, and one old man who had been with me on two or three occasions when I had followed up Isabeline and had thought me crazy for not having shot her instead of going miles and miles for the sake of 'looking' at her, was careful to inform me that it was not the mother with cubs that the villagers referred to.

It was June ere I got a chance of paying the dear old haunts a visit. Devil and Fool would now be 28 month's old and well able to look after themselves. Would I still be able to tell one from the other and when I did see them, would I forget all past associations and shoot on sight, or would I be as eager to watch their antics as of yore?

The second day after arriving on the scene, two bears were seen on a plateau some distance from camp, but too late in the evening to permit of my making a closer acquaintance on that day. Next morning I left camp before it was light and found myself far up on the highlands ere the first streaks of dawn touched the peaks ahead, and shortly after, my glasses revealed one solitary bear, and, if size was any criterion, the veteran who had done the damage among the flocks. Half an hour's careful talking brought me to within a few yards of where I had last seen him and a cautious look round showed him sitting on a patch of snow, meditating over his many misdeeds.

A low whistle roused him and he cocked his ears and peered round in the direction of the sound, but did not move his position. A depression in the ground served me admirably to run round and get in front of him, but he had heard me moving and was now on the alert though still sitting where I had left him. A snap shot was the work of a moment, and the monster's life blood dyed the white snow beneath him a bright crimson,

Later on I found Isabeline—alone. Devil and Fool had been driven from her side by the big beast whose hide now covers the floor, and the little mother roams the alpine pastures still, and has long forgotten the existence of her young hopefuls.

THE ELEPHANT AND THE CASSOWARY

Ruskin Bond

The baby elephant wasn't out of place in our home in north India because India is where elephants belong, and in any case our house was full of pets brought home by Grandfather, who was in the Forest Service. But the cassowary bird was different. No one had ever seen such a bird before—not in India, atleast. Grandfather had picked it up on a voyage to Singapore, where he'd been given the bird by a rubber planter who'd got it from a Dutch trader who'd got it from a man in Indonesia.

Anyway, it ended up, at our home in Dehra, seemed to do quite well in the sub-tropical climate. It looked like a cross between a turkey and an ostrich, but bigger than the former, and smaller than the latter—about five feet in height. It was not a beautiful bird, nor even a friendly one, but it had come to stay, and everyone was curious about it especially the baby elephants.

Right from the start the baby elephant took a great interest in the cassowary, a bird unlike any found in the Indian jungles.

'He would circle round the odd creature and diffidently examine with his trunk the texture of its stumpy wings; of course, he suspected no evil, and his childlike curiosity encouraged him to take liberties which resulted in an unpleasant experience.

'Noticing the baby elephant's attempts to make friends with the rather morose cassowary, we felt a bit apprehensive. Self-contained and sullen, the big bird responded only by slowly and slyly raising one of its powerful legs, in the meantime gazing into space with an innocent air. We knew what the gesture meant; we had seen that treacherous leg raised on many an occasion, and suddenly shooting out with a force that would have done credit to a vicious camel. In fact, camel and cassowary kicks are delivered in the same way, except that the camel kicks backward like a horse and the bird forward.

We wished to spare our baby elephant a painful experience, and led him away from the bird. But he persisted in his friendly overtures, and one morning he received an ugly reward. Rapid as lightning, the cassowary hit straight from the hip and knee joints, and the elephant ran squealing to Grandmother.

For several days he avoided the cassowary, and we thought he had learnt his lesson. He crossed and recrossed the compound and the garden, swinging his trunk, thinking furiously. Then, about a week later, he appeared on the veranda at breakfast-time in his usual cheery, childlike fashion, sidling up to the cassowary as if nothing had happened.

We were struck with amazement at this and so, it seemed, was the bird. Had the painful lesson already been forgotten, and by a member of the elephant tribe noted for its ability never to forget? Another dose of the same medicine would serve the baby right.

The cassowary once more began to draw up its fighting leg with sinister determination. It was nearing the true position for the master-kick, kung-fu style, when all of a sudden the baby elephant seized with his trunk the cassowary's other leg and pulled it down. There was a clumsy flapping of wings, a tremendous swelling of the bird's wattle, and an undignified getting up, as if it were a floored boxer doing his best to beat the count of ten. The bird then marched off with an attempt to look stately and unconcerned, while we at the breakfast-table were convulsed with laughter.

After this the cassowary bird gave the baby elephant as wide a berth as possible. But they were not forced to coexist for very long. The baby elephant, getting bulky and cumbersome, was sold and now lives in a zoological garden where he is a favourite with young visitors who love to take rides on his back.

As for the cassowary, he continued to grace our veranda for many years, gaped at, but not made much of, while entering on a rather friendless old age.

The Hindu, April 1993

THE PALE ONE

John Eyton

I

The Pale One was one of the most mysterious creatures in the world—a she-elephant, queen of her herd and of the vast jungles wherein they moved. Her kingdom stretched form the blue Nilgiri Hills, through leagues of rugged hillocks clothed in scrub, to the dense jungles on the Cauvery's banks. She and her kind had but little to do with the works of man, save for the occasional descent on a village at the jungle edge, when they would maraud a few fields for fodder; sometimes too in the dusk, on the Ootacamund road or on the way to Mercara, men would see great shadowy forms ahead of them, and would flee—but she was hardly aware of man at all.

Perhaps, her colour had attracted the great Tusker, who had wandered alone in the forests of Coorg until a bullet drove him from his old haunts into the jungle by the river. One evening, he saw the herd at drinking, and challenged at once, stamping and roaring and calling their ancient leader—the giant of the One Tusk—to battle; then all night he wandered round the bamboo brake, trumpeting defiance. In the morning the memorable battle started, which lasted three days and determined, in sight of all, the leadership of the herd. The jungle-folk kept away; even the tiger and the buffalo avoided the battle-ground, where trees were uprooted and pounded into the floor; where the very forest swayed to the movements of the fighters, while the cows trembled for their calves, and the young males stood aloof and envied the prowess. At last, height and great spirit won the victory over age and experience; the elephant of the One Tusk went alone and wounded from his kingdom, never to be seen again, while the great black Tusker danced the dance of victory and lorded it over the young males, and chose his bride.

She was of a paler grey than the rest, who were almost black, and her paleness came of an old stock, and won her his regard.

So, the Pale One knew her lord.

Who can tell of the wanderings of the herd during the three years which followed? They rarely stayed long in one place. In the rainy time they sought the hills, and in the dry time they followed the river, where they would stand at evening in the deep, draining great gulps, squirting one another, teaching the young to swim, revelling in the cool and depth of it. Great, black, shiny monsters they were, but by the side of the greatest of all was always one of paler hue, whom he served, towering over her with his immense height, full of tusk, broad of forehead, with great spreading ears. He ruled the twenty-five elephants of the herd sternly, nor brooked interference from other herds which crossed their path, so that they became famous, and had the freedom of all the jungles of the south, with the coolest places for the heat, the best drinking pools, and the sweetest bamboo groves. No elephant ever stood in the path of the big black Tusker, lord of the Pale One.

In the third summer of their wandering, directly after the rains, there came a spirit of unrest on the herd. They were leaving the hills for the country of green scrub and luscious fresh food, welcoming the sun, which they had not seen for many days. Yet, one day, as they stood basking in the open, a feeling of restlessness came on them. To an elephant this means either that he is in love or that he is being interfered with; in the latter case it is the instinct of the curtailment of that freedom which is his birthright. The old mother of the herd felt: it first, as it came on the breeze to her, and she communicated the news. They were not alone in the jungle; something was stirring between them and the hills—other elephants perhaps—or something unknown.

One or, two of the, younger males threw up their trunks and squealed, and were promptly dealt with by the Tusker, who wanted to listen, and said so; then shuffling and stamping ceased; mothers quieted their calves; only the breeze from the hills sighed in the grass and tiny birds twittered; then from faraway knowledge came to them.

The ground vibrated ever so slightly; other elephants were afoot…a great herd…two, three herds…one from the direction of the sun, another from the hills, and another from the plain of great grass. But there was something else…a new smell, vaguely disconcerting…men.

Then, an unusual thing happened: the big Tusker did not, as was his wont, turn to challenge the new herds, but began to move uneasily, aloof from the rest, throwing his trunk and shifting his feet; presently he moved slowly away, and the Pale title joined him; then, one by one, the rest followed. When they were together, the rush quickened to full pace, and they thrust through the thickets, massed like a wedge, driving a road over the country, never stopping till nightfall. It was a new experience—the first of many—and it meant panic. The herd had rarely travelled like that, at full pace, *en masse,* careless of its mothers and the calves...and never for a whole day. But they got beyond the area of unrest, and were in free land again, where the ground brought no vibrations, and the breeze no upsetting smell. They did not forget these things, because only a few things are forgotten by elephants, but they puzzled over them that night, and next day moved on towards the distant river jungles, not en *masse;* but in open feeding formation, eating as they went. For two days they travelled on over the low hillocks, each day making a longer midday halt; then, on the third day, they came upon a little pool with good green feeding on its banks, where they stayed a night and a day, carelessly feeding and wallowing. But at dusk they saw a new thing.

The older ones had seen it before, and thought little of it at a distance if they were hungry. What they saw was a line of little points of light, flashing out behind them, like stars over the hill; the wind brought smoke too, which tickled the trunk curiously; and there were little sounds, such as they had heard in villages; then a faint sound which they knew well—the far-off call of a she-elephant—the night call. Familiar it was, and yet unfamiliar; it brought back the spirit of unrest to them, for it was not a free call—it had trouble in it, such as they did not understand.

At the second trumpeting, the herd left the sucking mud and plunged into the darkness, careless of what they trampled or where they went, driving in fear through the night. From that time they knew restless days and nights; the sense of freedom had passed.

II

The twinkling lights were not those of a village, but of a great camp. There were a hundred campfires on the side of a low hill, and around them many inert squatted: The red glow lit up wild faces among the little tents and the trees; there was bustle of cooking and a good smell of hot food; pipes were being passed around from mouth to mouth, and in every group there was one who talked of elephants, and many who nodded. Here were grizzled old mahouts, heroes of many kheddahs,[1] who spoke of great elephants as if they were children, and wore the Maharajah's medals; their sons, smooth-faced young men in bright turbans, who hung upon their words; the elephant servants—thin, bearded Mohammedans, with sleepy, drugged eyes; the trackers—wild, hairy jungle men, almost naked, talking in strange tongues, and, besides, a motley crew of beaters and chamars[2] and water-carriers and coolies from Mysore and Malabar, who raised a babel of chatter. The only restful things were the lines of dim elephants in the background, silent for the most part, save when one trumpeted or brushed a branch to and fro with his trunk to clear it of dust. The fire flickers just showed these swaying forms under the trees, dignified amid the bustle, eating unhurriedly their heaps of green branches.

Meals were eaten; from some of the groups came snatches of song—the crooning of Southern love, and the triumphs of roping elephants, a drum was beaten in the shadows; then the talk died and men lay down, muffled in brown blankets, while the watchers sat silent. At last, there was no sound but the

---

[1] Kheddah = Enclosure.
[2] Chamar = Tanner, leather-worker.

shuffling and munching of the great sentinels of the moving camp, the driving elephants of Mysore.

There was, indeed, good cause for the panic of the wild herd. That moving camp was full of purpose, and the khaki-clad man with the eyes of a hunter, who ruled it, knew his business. This was the central camp of three, moving in the form of crescent over the elephant country, tracking herds, and persuading them gently forward day-by-day in the direction of the Cauvery Kheddahs. At present they were rounding up, but their most difficult duty lay ahead, and began with the exact timing of the last drive at close quarters when the three groups should converge on the same day. But it was all hard work, for they were moving in country untouched by man, far from villages and crops—the country of wild, elephant and buffalo. Their strange encounters in thicket and by river while driving or fetching chara[3] would fill many stories; but they were travelling all the time, tracking as they went, keeping touch with the other groups in a land of no communications, and rounding up stray elephants from the wild herds.

They had, made touch with three herds in all, and the biggest was in the middle. Only one man had seen this herd, which had moved forward like a phantom at full pace, and he spoke of a giant, a rajah among elephants, and of a pale tuskless elephant, standing out of the welter of the rest; the mighty mallan,[4] the torn-up trees; and the scarred tree-trunks on the elephant path showed that he spoke the truth, and that this was the master herd. By the time the three camps had converged in the neighbourhood of Karapur, where deep jungle flanks the Cauvery River, the Pale One and her lord had become

---

[3]Chara = Feed of elephants.
[4]Mallan = Track of an elephant.

famous, almost legendary…the theme of many a mahout's prayer and triumph-song. The herd had the reputation of being restless; as it was feared that they might overshoot the kheddah jungle and cross the river, they had not been over-harried or molested On the night before the kheddah drive they were tearing the bamboo near the river's edge, uneasy, but settled for the time being. There was a great suspense in the camp of two thousand men and two hundred elephants, gathered for the final act of their long drama.

III

Ever since the stampede from the pool the wild herd had travelled fast—too fast for the Pale One, who was shortly destined to present her lord with a son. More and more she had lagged behind, and only a great heart had helped her through. So, when at last they reached the welcome shade of the river jungle she lay down and rested long, while the others were tearing at the trees and rejoicing at having thrown off the unrest.

But they rejoiced too soon, for on the third day, as they were moving for the evening drink, they heard the trumpeting of an elephant near at hand, again and again, whereat the big Tusker stopped to listen; flapping his ears and gently raising his trunk. There were elephants close behind them…but not only elephants—there were men, many men. Sounds of drums and gongs and stirring and shouting filtered the trees as the herd fidgeted uneasily and began to mass. There was a moment of uncertainty, and then they saw lights in the wood, waving and bobbing, and waited to see no more, they crashed forward, shambling through the dense growth till they came out on to the stand by the river, where the red rays of the setting sun lit up the water and intensified the gloom of the farther bank…

then they plunged into the stream, the great Tusker leading and the Pale One in the rear, and between them a surge of scrambling subjects, old and young, half-grown and calves, fighting to gain the gloom of the bank beyond.

Then, suddenly that gloom burst into flame, Even the unconquerable drive of a wild herd was pulled up short. One moment all had been darkness and silence ahead of them; the next, men burst from the trees in hundreds with shouts and sudden noises like the rending of trees—and, above all, the lights. They could not face those torches. Dazed, bewildered, they turned upstream, to find that elephants had been put into the water from both banks and were advancing in line; the bank which they had left, too, was full of dancing, leaping men with lights. The herd hesitated; two young males broke away upstream and flung themselves against the line: it was like dashing against a brick wall. They met four great old Tuskers who pushed them squealing downstream with ugly blows in the ribs, while sharp spears pricked them in tender places from above, and loud cracks rang in their ears; smarting, buffeted, stunned, they blundered into the deep water with a gurgle and a splash, and half-swam, half-floundered past the herd, which was standing at bay. A black mass they made against the red sky—the humped forms gathered round the big Tusker, who with angry eyes, ears out, trunk extended, awaited the first shock.

Then, with a rush and a bump, the line met them; there was a mighty swaying and pushing—loud gun-shots, flashes, sharp thrusts, cries of men, smell of gunpowder—all in a melee; but the advancing line had the advantage of science, impetus, and the stream, and the wild herd had to give, breaking and scattering suddenly, the Pale One leading the rout. It was not her way to flee, but she knew that she must reserve her strength and trust her lord.

So the herd broke, but their spirit was not gone. Amid pandemonium from both banks there were a dozen individual fights as elephant after elephant broke back, leaving only the mothers with their calves to take their time and move on; but, one-by-one, they encountered new tactics, for they were cut off, roughly hustled, and mastered in detail, fight as they would. The big Tusker, who held the rear, found himself the special charge of four full-grown elephants; he could have tackled the lot in the open, unhampered, but here he was too angry for strategy; when he knocked one out of his way the other three butted into him from behind; and when he turned to vent his wrath he saw flashes and had stinging pains in the head. So, he could but lash and storm and ramp like a half-grown elephant, sending up the seater in great sprays around him, as he was gradually edged down below the steep right bank in the wake of the rest.

So, the herd was passing down the river, when suddenly the Pale One stood still. Below her, stretched across the stream, she saw another line—silent, impassive, motionless—of full forty elephants. She looked right and left; on the left the crowd still surged with their torches; on the right was the high bank—but here was a gap in the bank and a track into dark jungle above. Slowly and uncertainly she made for that gap, still suspicious, but, as nothing happened, she walked up the track, past a fence, into a bamboo grove. Then the herd, bundled together between two converging lines, massed again and followed their queen; last of all came the big Tusker, who stood proudly at bay in the middle of the gap. Then, a whole constellation of flashes dazed his eyes, and he, the lord of the Southern jungles, turned and followed his herd. Something clashed behind him—timber on timber. They were in kheddah.

IV

It was as if they had passed through a nightmare, and had awakened in good feeding jungle and absolute quiet. True, there were fires round the circle of the bamboo patch, and a jumble of sound, but they were not molested. The younger elephants started at once to feed on the bamboo, but the great Tusker remained aloof and sulky, touring round the patch and trying the defences. He found that they were surrounded by a ditch that could not be crossed and a timber fence that could not be reached, and his defiant trumpeting woke the echoes and told the herd that all was not well.

But the Pale One was beyond caring, for her time was very near. That night she went apart from the rest, and in the morning there lay beside her a little crumpled grey object no bigger than a sheep-dog. In the dim morning she stood over it, and caressed it with her trunk, till soon it tottered to its feet, and felt for her; so she fed it, forgetting the nightmare for a while.

For a day and a night they had peace, and she grew to love her little one at her side, playing with it, feeling all over it with her trunk, giving her milk freely for its strength, watching it find its feet.

Then, on the morning of the second day, the nightmare returned. The great Tusker, in his pilgrimage round the ditch, suddenly came face-to-face with a line of elephants drawn up outside for battle; he parted the bamboos, and for a long time remained gazing, measuring, taking stock...then slowly turned and rejoined the herd. Then they heard the opening of the gates and the entry of the enemy...so the great fight began.

They had good hope this time; they had rested and were in the open—their own ground; and they were prepared. The Pale

One went at once to a lonely corner, her little one ambling along at her side, while her lord led the charge in mass formation at the centre of the line. But, as they closed, the noises started again, and the pricks in tender parts, and all the bewilderments of the first fight. Once more they encountered science that was not of the wild, for they were deftly cut up and hustled in batches in the direction of a tall enclosure with a narrow entrance. Soon, it became evident that the strangers meant to drive them into that enclosure, and they resisted with might and main, breaking back again and again, scattering the enemy, they rallying to their leader...but always the enemy re-formed and encircled them. At noon honours were still equal, for the enemy retired outside, while the herd made for a muddy little swamp with shallow water in it, and for an hour drank deep for refreshment, and blew out spouts of muddy water to cool one another. Only the Pale One did not join them, tending her babe apart, ill at ease.

When the fight began again, the enemy had reinforced; the herd was completely surrounded in the swamp, and hustled pell-mell towards the enclosure, where a last stand was made against overwhelming numbers; nothing availed: willy-nilly they were bundled through the gap into the small enclosure, where they heaved and barged and squeezed, trumpeting and squealing, making the timbers creak.

Only the great Tusker managed to break away, irresistibly, as a ship drives through water, sending three elephants headlong before him. He stood near the gate, gathering his strength for an ugly rush, ready to take on the whole line in fair fight... But the fight was not fair; as he was advancing, there came the last indignity, and the first knowledge of slavery... the rope touched him. Deftly his head was lassoed; then a hind leg; then another; then came a mad struggle against six elephants tugging at the end of the ropes; he became aware of men too, and struggled more. The old freedom had gone; he could not fight devilry—creepers that twined and would not break. Dimly understanding that his hour had come, and that his birthright had been stolen from him, he suffered himself to be drawn away by the six down a steep bank into the cooling river...out of sight of his herd.

So passed the great Tusker into the haunts of men for the years of slavery.

It was the Pale One who made the Homeric fight, which will be told over campfires a generation hence. They found her in a corner, tending her babe, and she confronted them, pushing the babe beneath her body. Then they hemmed her in, but the trained elephants shrank from her and would not close, for all that she was the smaller and alone. Men said afterwards that she was bewitched, for she made the boldest half-hearted, and drove through them, butting with her broad forehead, striking with her heavy trunk. For an hour she led the hunt, and they could not catch her nor close with her; even when defeat seemed certain she broke the line with the force of a ram, and the boldest turned from her. She was fighting for more than life, or the honour of the herd, or the freedom of the South: she was battling for her young, and dimly she knew what the loss of the fight would mean—the loss of the love she felt for him.

She never would have been taken alive had she not looked down and missed her babe...saw it being led away...gave a mad squeal, and chased, with destruction in her eyes...then thundered against the great gates of the palisade.

So at last, they caught her easily enough. The Pale One had nothing more to fight for.

In the evening she stood alone under a tall tree, the chain

clanking at her leg. While the others trumpeted and fought their chains, she was silent, with an ineffable sadness. Pale and ghostly she loomed against the glow of the campfires, and men watched and wondered at her. Then, they brought her the little grey elephant-babe, which ran up to her and commanded milk with its tiny trunk....

The Pale One turned her head slowly away. The free days were past, and she would never know her babe again.

From *The Naked Fakir and Other Stories (1922)*

HUNTING WITH A CAMERA

F.W. Champion

On the left bank of the Ganges, a few miles below Lachmanjhula, in the United Provinces, where the holy river emerged from the Himalayan foothills, lies a great forest which forms the home of many wild beasts from the mighty elephant and tiger downwards. Hardwar, that sacred and populous Hindu city, is only a few miles away on the other side of the river, and the pious pilgrims who come from all over India to wash away their sins by bathing in the holy water little realize how often at night tigers stand on the opposite bank of the river to watch with curious gaze the bright illuminations of their festivals, or how these huge beasts even listen to the rumbling of the trains as they bring the pilgrims to the railway station after long journeys from all parts of India.

In this forest for many years has resided a very fine tigress, who has so far escaped destruction at the hands of the numerous sportsmen who are forever pursuing her—and may she continue to do so until old age mars her pleasure in the life which is as dear to her as their own is to her hunters! She is very powerfully built for a tigress and is perhaps as fine an example of her race as is to be found anywhere in northern India. For this reason the hunter who at last lays her low will undoubtedly feel very pleased with himself, although there are some amongst us—an increasing number these days, one is glad to be able to say—who can derive just as much pleasure from hunting with the bloodless camera, which, after all, takes no life and is much less selfish than shooting to kill, in that the resultant pictures can subsequently give pleasure to others in a way that skins or horns can never do even though the skin be stolen from one of the finest tigresses in northern India.

I will now describe a few episodes which have occurred from time to time during the last four or five years when we happened to be camping within this tigress' domain and have thus had opportunities to hunt her with a camera. The first time we became acquainted with her was several years ago, when she suddenly took to killing the buffaloes which the local bamboo-cutters use for dragging their produce down to the edge of the Ganges, where the bamboos are tied together into huge rafts and floated away to distant markets on the banks of the great Ganges canals—those fine monuments of the work of the Irrigation Department in Upper India. During a single week she killed four or five of these buffaloes and always left the carcases to be devoured by vultures after making one heavy meal. Several times, mounted on a tame elephant, we searched the places where we hoped she would be lying up during the day, but she was never there and it appeared that there were two reasons for this. Firstly, she had at the time two or three small cubs to feed, which meant that she had to kill more frequently than usual, whereas an attack of rinderpest had greatly reduced the numbers of the sambar which forms her usual food; and, secondly, she had been fired at in a beat and missed, so that she had learnt not to lie near her kills in the daytime. The result was that several natural kills produced no single glimpse of her to enable us to take a photograph, although one day a fine chital stag with his horns in velvet allowed us to approach within a few yards and seemed little perturbed at the click of the shutter as we recorded his picture. His very presence there, however, was a fairly certain indication that the tigress was not where we were hoping to find her. On another occasion, having once more failed to find our quarry, we followed a poor specimen of a sambar stag for two or three hours in the hope that he would stand in a good light and give us an opportunity to take his photograph; but he always moved too quickly from one belt of thick shade to another and all we could do was to snap him standing half-hidden among some bushes. Oh! if only the animal-photographer could explain to wild animals that, were they to stand out in the open for a few moments in a good pose, he would take their photographs, give them an honoured place on his wall or in his collection of jungle pictures and let them depart in peace!

But we are wandering from the subject of our tigress and must return. As we have already seen, she never seemed to be near her kills in the daytime and, as she generally left them in the open, they were usually devoured by jackals and vultures long before the evening. She soon gave up killing the dragging cattle, which was as well for her, because, although the loss of these cattle was largely due to the carelessness of their owners, who calmly left them loose at night in places which they knew the tigress might visit, I should otherwise have had to make an effort to destroy her in the interests of my forest employees. We then tried tying up young buffalo-baits in very quiet secluded spots; but we soon found that the only places where she would kill these baits were open cross-roads, which meant that hyenas and jackals—which frequent jungle roads—always smelt them out and fired off the automatic flashlight arranged over the kills early in the evening and long before there was any hope of the tigress arriving. One day she killed a bait in a particularly quiet spot, and, full of hope, we mounted on a tame elephant and stalked the kill very quietly in the heat of the afternoon. Sure enough, we found her at last dozing in the shade of a bamboo clump and thus obtained our first view of her magnificent proportions. But she was evidently sleeping with one eye open, for, although there was ample time for a quick shot with a rifle, she dashed off with an angry 'whoof' just as I was getting her into focus on the mirror of my reflex camera, so that once more she got the better of us. This particular kill, however, did not fail altogether as one of her cubs, who was by now three-parts grown, returned during the night and was caught by our automatic flashlight in the act of seizing the kill.

The next stage in our efforts to secure her photograph involved sitting out all night over a live-bait tied near an old kill, which we hoped would attract her to the spot and perhaps induce her to attack the living bait, over which the flashlight apparatus had been arranged during the daytime so that it could be fired by pulling a cord from the machan. The reader will now accompany me in thought to this machan and in imagination spend the night with me in the tree. We will assume that the difficult adjustments of the flashlight apparatus have already been done—they take several hours and we are now mounted on a tame elephant and approaching the chosen spot at about 4 p.m. on a fine warm afternoon. As we draw near the place, we move very slowly and approach carefully under cover, since tigers in general and this tigress in particular have a habit of doing the unexpected and who knows that we may now find her calmly eating her kill in broad daylight. But no: she is not here at the moment. A short distance from the old kill stands a dead tree on which are perched a number of vultures, evidently resting after their disgusting meal of putrid flesh, and above in the crystal clear sky, is circling a kite, also attracted by the prospect of food. We pause for a moment to watch the wonderful grace of the movements of his forked tail, which is a hundred-fold more efficient than the rudder of any ship or aeroplane invented by man, and then we move on again, noting as we approach the stealthy retreat of a pair of jackals, who have been stealing a meal during the absence of the rightful owner of the kill. We now climb up to the machan and, sending the elephant back to camp, settle down to the prospect of the deep enjoyment of a moonlight night spent absolutely alone in the heart of a great forest. All around us is a vast jungle containing no human being for miles in any direction, yet positively alive with wild animals and birds of every kind and description. Only a day or two previously a herd of about 20 wild elephants, including two or three tiny babies, passed under the very tree in which we are now sitting, and the place is notorious for sloth-bears, which come from long distances to feed on the luscious crop of berries now ripening on the *ber* bushes all around us. The local sambar have been sadly thinned out by a recent attack of rinderpest, but chital are common in the neighbourhood, which, among many other species, even holds a few of those curious four-horned antelope nowhere common in the Himalayan foothills. And the birds! Who can give any idea of the marvellous beauty and variety of the feathered denizens of the foothill forests? All around us are scores of peafowl, attracted like the bears by the ripening of the jungle fruits; green paroquets in hundreds are dashing about at a tremendous pace in every direction and screaming with joy in harsh raucous tones as though they are revelling in the thrill of their rapid motion through the air; bulbuls are twittering on almost every bush; plover of two or three species are running about the dry sandy *rau* bed in front of us; two or three kites are screaming in the air above us; a pair of fantailed flycatchers are pirouetting from twig to twig of the very tree in which we are sitting; and a host of others of every conceivable shape and colours are to be seen and heard in all directions. All seem bubbling over with a happiness which finds ready expression in song and play. And yet some naturalists claim that all Nature is intensely cruel? Those of us, however, who enjoy watching rather than destroying wild creatures do not find Nature cruel—far from it. Sudden death appears at intervals, it is true, but it is only our vivid imagination and fear of the hereafter that make us afraid of death. Wild creatures do not know what death is and are not troubled by thoughts about Heaven and Hell, so that the sudden passing of one of their number as the result of the advent of some flesh-eating animal or bird is but a fleeting incident soon forgotten by the survivors. But once again we are straying from our subject.

We sit happily on in our machan, hoping against hope that at last the tigress will give us our chance to take her photograph and imperceptibly the day passes away to be replaced by the full glory of a jungle night. Once or twice we hear the alarm cry of a kakar or chital in the distance and hope surges up in our hearts, only to die down again as the cries soon cease. Then a curious rumbling comes from the direction of Hardwar, some distance away, and we wonder what *tamasha* there can be making such a disturbance. But the noise seems to be increasing, and, at last, straining over the edge of the machan, we realize with dismay that a heavy storm is rapidly approaching from the west. What are we to do? We have no mackintosh and little bedding and our camp is several miles away, with a jungle full of wild beasts in between and no lamp or path to help us get there. Yet if we stay in the *machan* we are bound to get wet through and thoroughly chilled, which will inevitably result in a bout of fever. Even as we consider the problem the moon disappears, dazzling lightning flashes across the sky in all directions, a strong wind begins to blow, and down comes a tropical deluge of rain which soon soaks the camera, flashlight, blankets, and finally us. All hope of our long-sought picture has gone, and, feeling distinctly nervous of being struck by lighting, we see in imagination our tigress hugging herself with glee at the thought of how well we are being punished for having had the impertinence to continue for so long in the vain pursuit of her photograph. At long last, after we have become resigned to spending a night of misery, we hear a curious whistling which does not seem to come from any animal or bird we recognize. Surely we are not beginning to get a little light in the head as a result of our nerve-racking experience? No the whistling continues and increases in volume so that at last we realize, with a thrill of joy, that it must be one of our tame elephants, which, despite our orders to the contrary, has been sent out by my wife to rescue us from our predicament. We eagerly call up the elephant, thankful to escape from our chilly damp perch, and rapidly return to our comfortable camp 4 miles away, which we reach at about 1 a.m. Shortly afterwards, fortified by hot Bovril, we are dozing in a comfortable warm bed and dreaming of new schemes for obtaining the photograph which had now become a fetish with us.

Thus the campaign continued for some years, but always without success. We could never find her again by stalking in the daytime; she always seemed to discover our presence if we sat in machans over her kills at night; and, if we arranged our automatic flashlight apparatus over her kills, she waited until hyenas and jackals had spent some time there first and thus fired the flashlight before she was due to appear. It seemed as though she were going to win in this contest of wits, and then, at last, we had a brilliant idea. We had a kill one day on the edge of a broad *rau* bed and we had noticed previously, from a study of her tracks, that she had formed the habit of hugging the foot of a low bank on the edge of this *rau* bed when passing this particular locality. How would it be if we were to arrange a tripwire at the edge of this bank, some distance from the kill, and thus avoid the risk of the chance being ruined by the inevitable jackals and hyenas? There seemed some hope of this method proving successful, especially as we had a good idea of the direction from which she was likely to arrive and could thus probably guide her, all unconsciously, by means of a judicious arrangement of cut branches, to the exact spot where our photographic trap was to be set. We decided to carry out this plan and arranged our apparatus with extreme care, even to the last detail of a trip-wire carefully matched to the colour of the surrounding ground for she had seen one of our trip-wires once before and carefully stepped over it without touching it! We then returned to our camp with a sneaking hope that at long last we stood a fair chance of winning in the long-drawn-out battle of wits. About midnight we heard the familiar boom of the exploding flashlight and we were so excited that we jumped out of bed and hurried out to the spot by the light of a lantern. Had we really succeeded at last, or had those…hyenas and jackals once more ruined a good chance? After what seemed a tremendous time, although in reality the distance was quite short, we at last reached the spot and—hurrah? There were the tell-tale claw marks in the gound as she had involuntarily extended her claws on being startled by the noise and light of the exploding flashlight. Yes: the complicated mechanism of tripping the shutter had also worked without a hitch—it does not always do so—and at last our plate had been exposed. Now for the final stage of development. We rushed back to our camp, and, although it was the middle of the night, out came the developing chemicals, and before many minutes had passed we had the tremendous satisfaction of seeing a fine negative appearing in the developing dish—a negative which, except for a slight fault in one of the fore-legs, is as good as we had ever hoped to obtain even in our most optimistic moments.

Thus ended the hunt for the first negative of this fine tigress, to whom we take off our hats with heartfelt thanks for having given us such a fine run for our money. We could have shot her years before when we first saw her, and, had we done so, all would have been over except for a skin which would have begun rotting away by now under the effects of this trying climate. Yet she lives on and may still provide us with more harmless pleasure, so who can now say that, once we have overcome our primitive and savage lust of killing, hunting with a camera is not the peer of any form of blood-hunting that the world can produce.

THE LIFE OF A TIGER

S. Eardley-Wilmot

As time went on the solitude which at first had been so marked a feature in the tiger's domain was broken by the ever-increasing number of human beings who found occupation or amusement therein. Formerly, only herds of cattle and their attendants roamed the forest, paying no attention to the jungle-folk, and were hardly noticed by them; later on came those who felled timber and cut bamboos, their camps were numerous all over the area; and last of all came the hunting parties of varying size, from the solitary sportsman who wandered afoot amongst the wild animals, to the large company, well organized to slay, who boasted of the number of their victims, and were proud of their stud of elephants and of their army of trackers and huntsmen. Not only peace but safety had departed, for though the graziers might not tell of the tiger's whereabouts, there were others, cartmen, sawyers and carpenters, who for the sake of a small reward, indeed often as a remedy for their own fears, would report all that they saw or heard to those who were able to make use of the information.

The tiger, now well experienced and cautious, gifted moreover with a most intimate acquaintance with the forest, yet found difficulty in evading all of these human beings, and their repeated invasions so seriously reduced the head of game in his hunting grounds, and forced the remainder to be so constantly on the alert that he lived in a perpetual state of anxiety, and was often put to great trouble before he could obtain a meal. Even when he had succeeded in capturing his prey, he feared to return to the kill lest during his absence some ambush should have been laid; so that, unless he could drag his victim close to some water supply, he derived but one day's food from even the largest animal. For tigers must drink after a heavy meal of flesh, and particularly in the hot weather when hunting parties were abroad, he suffered torments if forced to remain thirsty for many hours.

He dreaded the approach of human beings and the loud reports of the weapons they carried; and so while eager to slink away if this were possible, yet, if by chance his retreat was cut off, his natural courage asserted itself, and was indeed fortified by his hatred of his persecutors. He had seen others fall victims to the dangers he had so far escaped; the stag with mortal wound rushing blindly through the forest only to fall dead when breasting the stony slopes; or the panther lying harmless after hours of agony; he had followed the trail of others, doomed to a lingering death but for his swift interference; and the increasing difficulties of his existence rendered him more cautious and also more morose. For to live always in fear of death results in a change of habits and characteristics, and induces a strain of unaccustomed cruelty. He had been driven by gangs of beaters, and had learned that the less risk lay in escaping through the advancing line; for, though there might be guns there, yet, in the confusion of his onslaught, these had hitherto been ineffective; while the very caution necessary to steal away through the hidden sportsmen in front afforded to these an easy shot from their posts of vantage. He had been fired at from machans, and now was reluctant to take the risk of appropriating the baits of young buffaloes which he frequently came across; and, whereas formerly he expected no danger to lurk in the trees above him, now the need for circumspection was doubled by the possibility of a hunter being hidden in any leafy tree.

The tiger lay one night on the borders of a jungle clearing where the unfertile soil was covered with a growth of thorny bushes, which assumed strange shapes in the transparent gloom of the night. He had come for miles through the darker forest, moving slowly with the greatest circumspection; at each footstep the soft-padded paws seemed to feel the earth before any weight was allowed to bear on them; mechanically in their descent they pushed softly aside any dry leaf or twig which might, by their crackling, give notice of movement in the jungle, and now, tired from the constant nervous strain, he was resting before resuming his solitary way. A movement in the fantastic outlines of the bushes caught his attention, and he shrank still further into the friendly earth, all his fears at once aroused. A family of sloth-bears were feeding on the wild berries, embracing the bushes with shaggy arms, tearing off the fruit, intermingled with leaves and twigs, in the rough manner common to these beasts.

The tiger was glad even of this companionship, for it suffered him to relax his attention, for bears have the keenest power of scent, relying on this rather than on hearing or sight, so that timely warning of any intruder would be given.

The bears roamed round the little clearing, leaving no bush till despoiled of the fruit it bore, then commenced digging for roots and snuffing at the anthills to discover whether or not these were in occupation. The male bear soon found one to his liking, and commenced digging with his powerful claws to force an entry to the main passage, while the mother and her cubs sat around regarding the proceedings, though they could not possibly expect any share in the spoils. By dint of hard labour the bear had dug some three feet below the surface of the soil, and now inserting his muzzle in the tunnel drew deep inhalations which dragged with them crowds of unwilling insects into the moist mouth which was ready to receive them. The bear presented a ludicrous sight with his head buried in the earth and his hindquarters raised high towards the sky, and the noise of his breathing sounded loud through the still forest. After a time he commenced again to dig till he reached the nest, with its paper-like combs full of helpless maggots, and this he devoured in great mouthfuls. Then, while enjoying this selfish meal, he suddenly caught the scent of the tiger in the night air, and as quickly turned to fly. In his clumsy way he stumbled against the she-bear, and she, with the prompt retaliation of her tribe, at once struck and bit at her mate. Immediately the forest re-echoed with loud discordant cries, and the whole family disappeared into the forest, biting and scratching, in the belief that some enemy was amongst them seeking their lives.

The tiger wandered onwards through the jungle. He was now a different animal to what he had been in the days of his youth, when food was plentiful and danger not incessant. Now, for no fault of his own, he was proscribed; a price was set on his head, he was fired at on sight, and the very scarcity of food was used as a means to lure him to destruction. He was forced to satisfy his hunger by means he had formerly despised. He would lie by the drinking pools in the hot weather and ambush the jungle tribes while they were quenching an intolerable thirst; he would follow the females encumbered by the care of their young and profit by their maternal instincts to slay them; and would drive less powerful animals off their 'kills' and appropriate the spoil.

Domestic cattle he killed without mercy, so that he was known and dreaded throughout the countryside; he was always fierce and morose because he was at war with mankind, who had robbed him of his hunting grounds and with them of his means of living and of his contentment.

It was in these unhappy circumstances that his second courtship began, but on this occasion he forced a fight on his rival; for in the first place he was more savage than of old, and in the second it could not be tolerated that another should hunt in a forest where food was already but too scarce. Thus, ill-temper and fear of dispossession urged him more than passion and in result there was a combat unique in its ferocity. There was no interruption from human beings, as these had mostly left the forest at the commencement of the malarial season, and the few foresters who remained were careful not to approach the spot whence the sound of the struggle proceeded.

The opponents were well matched, for what the stranger yielded in weight he gained in agility, and any deficiency in experience was outweighed by his impetuosity. The two rushed furiously at each other, meeting with a shock that seemed to compel them to stand upright, and in that position each tried to grip the other's throat and was repulsed by the powerful claws which scratched deep into the flesh. They retreated breathless, again and again to renew the attack after lengthening intervals; meanwhile the earth was trodden down and became slippery with moisture, though scored by the sharp claws of the hind-feet of the combatants. It was after many rounds had been fought, without marked advantage to either side, though both had received painful wounds, that the tiger slipped as he was repelling a specially violent onslaught by the stranger, and, over-borne, was hurled on to his back. In an instant the other rushed in to end the fray with teeth buried in the chest or throat of his foe; and here he made the mistake which cost him his life. He should have waited for the defenceless moment when the other was attempting to rise, instead of attacking him when in a position assumed by all the cat-tribe in moments of difficulty. And so it was that, before a grip could be secured, the stranger's head and neck were seized in a vice and at the same time his belly was ripped open by the hind-claws of his prostrate foe. His only wish was to be free of this deadly embrace, and at last he was allowed to stagger away mortally wounded. The crushing blow which followed seemed to drive the life out of him, and he had no feeling for the fangs which penetrated heart and lungs. The tiger lay long by his defeated rival; he was marked with scars which lasted to his dying day, he was sore with bruises and bites, and weak in everything but ill-temper and ferocity. It might have been better for him if he had ended his life at this time, if he had assumed no fresh domestic responsibilities, for the future was to bring even more bitterness than the past.

From *The Life of a Tiger* by S. Eardley-Wilmot, C.I.E.

THE MAN-EATER OF BOTTA SINGARUM

Henry Astbury Leveson

I was hunting in the Deccan, in the neighbourhood of Mulkapore, when I heard that a man-eating tiger, which I had been after for some days, had been seen skulking near the outskirts of the village of Botta Singarum. I had on a former occasion tracked this cunning brute to one of his lairs, where the remains of several of his victims were discovered, and had twice beaten all his usual haunts in the jungle; but up to this time had never been able to get a shot at him. Sending my gang of trackers on before I mounted my horse, and guided by the villager who brought the news, I made my way to the place where the marauder had been seen the evening before, where I found unmistakable signs that the information I had received was true, as his fresh pugs were plainly visible.

I sent my horse back to the village, and accompanied by the gang, followed his track through a narrow ravine densely wooded tract. Here the trail became exceedingly difficult to follow, as the brute had evidently been walking about backwards and forwards in the bed and along the banks of a dry nullah, and we could not distinguish his last trail. I caused the band to separate, and for half an hour or so we were wandering about as if in a maze, for the cunning brute had been describing circles, and often by following the trail, we arrived at the place we started from.

Whilst we were all at a loss, suddenly I heard a low 'coo' twice repeated, and I knew that Googooloo, who was seldom at fault, was now on warm scent, and from his call I was as certain that the game was afoot as any master of hounds would have been, while breaking cover, to hear his favourite dog give tongue. The gang closed up, and guided by the sound, we made our way through thick bush to where Googooloo was standing by a pool of water in the bed of the nullah.

Here were unmistakable marks of his having quenched his thirst quite lately, for when we came up the water was still flowing into the deeply-imprinted pugs of his fore feet, which were close to the edge of the pool, and I noticed that the water had still the appearance of having been disturbed and troubled. After having drunk, the brute made his way to some very thick jungle, much overgrown with creepers, through which we could not follow without the aid of our axes. Thus stalking with any hope of success was out of the question, so I held a solemn consultation with Kistimah, Chineah, Googooloo, and the *dhoby,* as to the best means of proceeding.

I felt convinced that the brute was still lurking somewhere near at hand in the jungle, for, besides the very recent trail we were on, I fancied I heard the yelling of a swarm of monkeys, which I attributed to their having been frightened by his appearance; besides, this was just the kind of place where a tiger would be likely to remain in during the heat of the day, as it afforded cool shade from the sun, and water. All the gang were of my opinion, and Kistimah observed that, on two different occasions, after a post-runner had been carried off, he had remarked that the trail of the tiger led from this part of the jungle to a bend in the road, where he had been known frequently to lie in wait for his prey. 'These man-eaters,' he added, 'are great devils and *very* cunning, and I should not at all wonder if even now he was watching us from some dark thicket.' As he said this I carefully examined the caps of my rifle, and I observed some of the gang close up with a strange shudder, for this brute had inspired them all with a wholesome fear, and prevented their straggling. Two or three spoke almost in whispers, as if they were afraid of his really being sufficiently near to hear them conspiring for his destruction.

At length Kistimah said that he had been thinking of a plan which, though dangerous in the execution, might be attended with success. It was for me to go, with a man dressed as a runner, down the main road at sunset, being the time the tiger generally carried off his victims, and to run the chance of getting a shot. At this proposition sundry interjectional expressions, such as 'Abah!' 'Arrez!' 'Tuba!' 'Toba!' escaped from the lips of the bystanders, and from sundry shaking of heads and other unmistakable signs, I could see that it had not found much favour in their eyes. Chineah, the dhoby, and one or two of the gang, however, approved of the plan, and Kistimah offered to accompany me as the post-runner. This, however, I objected for I thought I should have a better chance of meeting the tiger if I went alone than in company; besides, I preferred having only myself to look after. The plan of action once settled, I returned to the village and obtained from the Patel the bamboo on which the tappal-runners sling the mailbags over their shoulders. To the end of this is an iron ring with a number of small pieces of metal attached, making a jingling noise as the man runs, which gives warning of the coming of the post to any crowd that might be obstructing the path, allowing them time to get out of his way. Having broken off the ring, I fastened it to my belt, so as to allow it to jingle as I walked, and arming myself with a short double rifle by Westley Richards, a brace of pistols, and a huge shekar knife, I made Kistimah lead the way down the road towards the place where the man-eater was said to lurk.

About a mile from the village I made the gang and the villagers who accompanied me halt, and went on with Kistimah, Chineah, and Googooloo to reconnoitre the ground. The road was intersected by a narrow valley or ravine, along the bottom of which was a dry, sandy watercourse, the banks of which were overgrown with high rank grass and reeds, intermixed with low scrubby thorn-bushes. To the left was a low rocky hill, in some place bare and in others covered with thick jungle, with wild date or custard-apple clumps here and there. Kistimah pointed me out a clump of rather thick jungle to the right of the road, where, he said, the tiger often lurked whilst on the look-out for his prey, and here we saw two or three old trails. He also showed me a rock, from behind which the brute had sprung upon a post-runner some weeks before; but we saw no signs of his having been there lately. It was, however, quite what an Indian sportsman would term a 'tigerish-looking spot', for bold, scarped rocks, and naked, fantastic peaks rose in every direction from amongst the dense foliage of the surrounding jungle, whilst here and there noble forest trees lowered like giant patriarchs above the lower verdure of every shade and colour.

Not a breath of air was stirring nor a leaf moving, and as the sun was still high up, without a cloud visible to intercept his rays, the heat was most oppressive, and even respiration become difficult on account of a peculiar closeness arising from the decayed vegetation underfoot, and the overpowering perfume of the blossoms of certain jungle plants.

Having reconnoitred the ground round about, I felt rather overcome with lassitude, and returned to the rest of the gang whom I found sleeping in a clump of deep jungle a little off the roadside. Here I lay down to rest, protected from the piercing rays of the sun by the shade of a natural bower formed by two trees, which were bent down with the weight of an immense mass of parasitical plants in addition to their own foliage. I must have slept several hours, for when I awoke I found the sun sinking low in the horizon; however, I got up considerably refreshed by my nap, and giving myself a shake, prepared for the task I had undertaken. I carefully examined my arms, and having ascertained that nothing had been seen by any of my gang, some of whom had kept a look-out, I told my people that if they heard the sound of my gun they might come up, otherwise they were to remain quiet where they were until my return. I ordered Chineah, Kistimah, Googooloo, and the dhoby, to accompany me down the road with spare guns in case I might want them; and when I arrived at a spot which commanded a view of the ravine which was supposed to be the haunt of the man-eater, I sent them to climb different trees.

Kistimah begged hard to be allowed to accompany me, as he said this tiger never attacked a man in front, but always from behind; but I would not permit him, as I thought that two people would perhaps scare the animal, and his footsteps might prevent me from hearing any sound intimating his approach.

The sun had almost set as I proceeded slowly down the road, and although I was perfectly cool and as steady as possible, I felt cold drops of perspiration start from my forehead as I approached the spot where so many victims had been sacrificed. I passed the rock, keeping well on the look-out, listening carefully for the slightest sound, and I remember feeling considerably annoyed by the chirping made by a couple of little bulbuls, that were fighting in a bush close to the roadside. Partridges were calling loudly all around, and as I passed the watercourse I saw a jackal skulking along its bed. I stopped, shook my jingling affair, and listened several times as I went along, but to no purpose.

Whilst ascending the opposite side of the ravine I heard a slight noise like the crackling of a dry leaf. I paused, and turning to the left fronted the spot from whence I thought the noise proceeded. I distinctly saw a movement or waving in the high grass, as if something was making its way towards me; then I heard a loud purring sound, and saw something twitching backwards and forwards behind a clump of low bush and long grass, about eight or ten paces from me, and a little in the rear. It was a ticklish moment, but I felt prepared. I stepped back a couple of paces in order to get a better view, which probably saved my life, for immediately the brute sprang into the middle of the road, alighting about 6 feet from the place where I was standing. I fired a hurried shot ere he could gather himself up for another spring, and when the smoke cleared away I saw him rolling over and over in the dusty road, writhing in his death agony, for my shot had entered the neck and gone downwards into his chest. I stepped on one side and gave him my second barrel behind the ear, when dark blood rushed from his nostrils, a slight tremor passed over all his limbs, and all was still. The man-eater was dead, and his victims avenged.

My gang, attracted by the sound of my shots, came rushing up almost breathless, and long and loud were the rejoicings when the tiger was recognized by Kistimah as the cunning man-eater who had been the scourge of the country for months. He was covered with mange, and but had little hair left on his skin, which was of a reddish brown colour, and not worth taking.

I have killed many tigers both before and since, but I never met with such a determined enemy to mankind, for he was supposed to have carried off more than a hundred individuals. He fully exemplified an old Indian saying: 'When a tiger has once tasted human blood he will never follow other game, men proving an easier prey.' On the spot where the tiger was killed a large mausoleum now stands, caused by the passers-by each throwing a stone until a large heap is formed. Since that day many a traveller who passed that way have been entertained by the old pensioned sepoy, who is in charge of the travellers' bungalow, with an account of the terrible man-eater of Botta Singarurn.

This account on the death of a man-eater in Botta Singarum (a village near Malkapur in the Telangana region), is taken from Henry Astbury Leveson's famous book, Sport in Many Lands. *His other well-known books are:* The Hunting Grounds of the Old World *(1860) and* The Forest and the Field *(1867). Henry Astbury Leveson (1828-75) was considered among the foremost of big-game hunters.*

Henry Astbury Leveson, the Old Shekarrey, 1877

THE EYE OF THE EAGLE

Ruskin Bond

It was a high, piercing sound, almost like the yelping of a dog. Jai stopped picking the wild strawberries, that grew in the grass around him, and looked up at the sky. He had a dog—a shaggy guard-dog called Motu—but Motu did not yet yelp, he growled and barked. The strange sound came from the sky, and Jai had heard it before. Now, realizing what it was, he jumped to his feet, calling to his dog, calling his sheep to start for home. Motu came bounding towards him, ready for a game.

'Not now, Motu!' said Jai. 'We must get the lambs home quickly.' Again he looked up at the sky.

He saw it now, a black speck against the sun, growing larger as it circled the mountain, coming lower every moment—a Golden Eagle, king of the skies over the higher Himalayas, ready now to swoop and seize its prey.

Had it seen a pheasant or a pine marten? Or was it after one of the lambs? Jai had never lost a lamb to an eagle, but recently some of the other shepherds had been talking about a golden eagle that had been preying on their flocks.

The sheep had wandered some way down the side of the mountain, and Jai ran after them to make sure that none of the lambs had gone off on its own.

Motu ran about, barking furiously. He wasn't very good at keeping the sheep together—he was often bumping into them and sending them tumbling down the slope—but his size and bear-like look kept the leopards and wolves at a distance.

Jai was counting the lambs; they were bleating loudly and staying close to their mothers. *One-two-three-four...*

There should have been a fifth. Jai couldn't see it on the slope below him. He looked up towards a rocky ledge near the steep path to the Tung temple. The golden eagle was circling the rocks.

The bird disappeared from sight for a moment, then rose again with a small creature grasped firmly in its terrible talons.

'It has taken a lamb!' shouted Jai. He started scrambling up the slope. Motu ran ahead of him, barking furiously at the big bird as it glided away over the tops of the stunted junipers to its eyrie on the cliffs above Tung.

There was nothing that Jai and Motu could do except stare helplessly and angrily at the disappearing eagle. The lamb had died the instant it had been struck. The rest of the flock seemed unaware of what had happened. They still grazed on the thick, sweet grass of the mountain slopes.

'We had better drive them home, Motu,' said Jai, and at a nod from the boy, the big dog bounded down the slope, to take part in his favourite game of driving the sheep homewards. Soon he had them running all over the place, and Jai had to dash about trying to keep them together. Finally they straggled homewards.

'A fine lamb gone,' said Jai to himself gloomily. 'I wonder what Grandfather will say.'

Grandfather said, 'Never mind. It had to happen some day. That eagle has been watching the sheep for some time.'

Grandmother, more practical, said, 'We could have sold the lamb for three hundred rupees. You'll have to be more careful in future, Jai. Don't fall asleep on the hillside, and don't read storybooks when you are supposed to be watching the sheep!'

'I wasn't reading this morning,' said Jai truthfully, forgetting to mention that he had been gathering strawberries.

'It's good for him to read,' said Grandfather, who had never had the luck to go to school. In his days, there weren't any schools in the mountains. Now there was one in every village.

'Time enough to read at night,' said Grandmother, who did not think much of the little one-room school down at Maku, their home village.

'Well, these are the October holidays,' said Grandfather. 'Otherwise he would not be here to help us with the sheep. It will snow by the end of the month, and then we will move with the flock. You will have more time for reading then, Jai.'

At Maku, which was down in the warmer valley, Jai's parents tilled a few narrow terraces on which they grew barley, millets and potatoes. The old people brought their sheep up to the Tung meadows to graze during the summer months. They stayed in a small stone hut just off the path which pilgrims took to the ancient temple. At 12,000 feet above sea level, it was the highest Hindu temple on the inner Himalayan ranges.

The following day Jai and Motu were very careful. They did not let the sheep out of sight even for a minute. Nor did they catch sight of the golden eagle. 'What if it attacks again?' wondered Jai. 'How will I stop it?'

The great eagle, with its powerful beak and talons, was more than a match for boy or dog. Its hind claw, four inches round the curve, was its most dangerous weapon. When it spread its wings, the distance from tip to tip was more than eight feet.

The eagle did not come that day because it had fed well and was now resting in its eyrie. Old bones, which had belonged to pheasants, snow-cocks, pine martens and even foxes, were scattered about the rocks which formed the eagle's home. The eagle had a mate, but it was not the breeding season and she was away on a scouting expedition of her own.

The golden eagle stood on its rocky ledge, staring majestically across the valley. Its hard, unblinking eyes missed nothing. Those strange orange-yellow eyes could spot a field-rat or a mouse-hare more than a hundred yards below.

There were other eagles on the mountain, but usually they kept to their own territory. And only the bolder ones went for lambs, because the flocks were always protected by men and dogs.

The eagle took off from its eyrie and glided gracefully, powerfully over the valley, circling the Tung mountain.

Below lay the old temple, built from slabs of grey granite. A line of pilgrims snaked up the steep, narrow path. On the meadows below the peak, the sheep grazed peacefully, unaware of the presence of the eagle. The great bird's shadow slid over the sunlit slopes.

The eagle saw the boy and the dog, but he did not fear them. He had his eye on a lamb that was frisking about on the grass, a few feet away from the other grazing sheep.

Jai did not see the eagle until it swept round an outcrop of rocks about a hundred feet away. It moved silently, without any movement of its wings, for it had already built up the momentum for its dive. Now it came straight at the lamb.

Motu saw the bird in time. With a low growl he dashed forward and reached the side of the lamb at almost the same instant that the eagle swept in.

There was a terrific collision. Feathers flew. The eagle screamed with rage. The lamb tumbled down the slope, and Motu howled in pain as the huge beak struck him high on the leg.

The big bird, a little stunned by the clash, flew off rather unsteadily, with a mighty beating of its wings.

Motu had saved the lamb. It was frightened but unhurt. Bleating loudly, it joined the other sheep, who took up the bleating. Jai ran up to Motu, who lay whimpering on the ground. There was no sign of the eagle. Quickly he removed his shirt and vest; then he wrapped his vest round the dog's wound, tying it in position with his belt.

Motu could not get up, and he was much too heavy for Jai to carry. Jai did not want to leave his dog alone, in case the eagle returned to attack.

He stood up, cupped his hand to his mouth, and began calling for his Grandfather.

'Dada, dada!' he shouted, and presently Grandfather heard him and came stumbling down the slope. He was followed by another shepherd, and together they lifted Motu and carried him home.

Motu had a bad wound, but Grandmother cleaned it and applied a paste made of herbs. Then she laid strips of carrot over the wound—an old mountain remedy—and bandaged the leg. But it would be some time before Motu could run about again. By then it would probably be snowing and time to leave these high-altitude pastures and return to the valley. Meanwhile, the sheep had to be taken out to graze, and Grandfather decided to accompany Jai for the remaining period.

They did not see the golden eagle for two or three days, and, when they did, it was flying over the next range. Perhaps it had found some other source of food, or even another flock of sheep. Are you afraid of the eagle?' Grandfather asked Jai.

'I wasn't before,' said Jai. 'Not until it hurt Motu. I did not know it could be so dangerous. But Motu hurt it too. He banged straight into it!'

'Perhaps it won't bother us again,' said Grandfather thoughtfully. 'A bird's wing is easily injured—even an eagle's.'

Jai wasn't so sure. He had seen it strike twice, and he knew that it was not afraid of anyone. Only when it learnt to fear his presence would it keep away from the flock.

The next day Grandfather did not feel well; he was feverish and kept to his bed. Motu was hobbling about gamely on three legs; the wounded leg was still very sore.

'Don't go too far with the sheep,' said Grandmother. 'Let them graze near the house.'

'But there's hardly any grass here,' said Jai.

'I don't want you wandering off while that eagle is still around.'

'Give him my stick,' said Grandfather from his bed. Grandmother took it from the corner and handed it to the boy. It was an old stick, made of wild cherry wood, which Grandfather often carried around. The wood was strong and well-seasoned; the stick was stout and long. It reached upto Jai's shoulders.

'Don't lose it,' said Grandfather. 'It was given to me many years ago by a wandering scholar who came to the Tung temple. I was going to give it to you when you got bigger, but perhaps this is the right time for you to have it. If the eagle comes near you, swing the stick around your head. That should frighten it off!'

Clouds had gathered over the mountains, and a heavy mist hid the Tung temple. With the approach of winter, the flow of pilgrims had been reduced to a trickle. The shepherds had started leaving the lush meadows and returning to their villages at lower altitudes. Very soon the bears and the leopards and the golden eagles would have the high ranges all to themselves.

Jai used the cherry wood stick to prod the sheep along the path until they reached the steep meadows. The stick would have to be a substitute for Motu. And they seemed to respond to it more readily than they did to Motu's mad charges.

Because of the sudden cold and the prospect of snow, Grandmother had made Jai wear a rough woollen jacket and a pair of high boots bought from a Tibetan trader. He wasn't used to the boots—he wore sandals at other times—and had some difficulty in climbing quickly up and down the hillside. It was tiring work, trying to keep the flock together. The cawing of some crows warned Jai that the eagle might be around, but the mist prevented him from seeing very far.

After some time the mist lifted and Jai was able to see the temple and the snow-peaks towering behind it. He saw the golden eagle, too. It was circling high overhead. Jai kept close to the flock—one eye on the eagle, one eye on the restless sheep.

Then the great bird stooped and flew lower. It circled the temple and then pretended to go away. Jai felt sure it would be back. And a few minutes later it reappeared from the other side of the mountain. It was much lower now, wings spread out and back, taloned feet to the fore, piercing eyes fixed on its target—a small lamb that had suddenly gone frisking down the slope, away from Jai and the flock.

Now it flew lower still, only a few feet off the ground, paying no attention to the boy.

It passed Jai with a great rush of air, and as it did so the boy struck out with his stick and caught the bird a glancing blow.

The eagle missed its *prey*, and the tiny lamb skipped away.

To Jai's amazement, the bird did not fly off. Instead it landed on the hillside and glared at the boy, as a king would glare at a humble subject who had dared to pelt him with a pebble.

The golden eagle stood almost as tall as Jai. Its wings were still outspread. Its fierce eyes seemed to be looking through and through the boy.

Jai's first instinct was to turn and run. But the cherry wood stick was still in his hands, and he felt sure there was power in it. He saw that the eagle was about to launch itself again at the lamb. Instead of running away, he ran forward, the stick raised above his head.

The eagle rose a few feet off the ground and struck out with its huge claws.

Luckily for Jai, his heavy jacket took the force of the blow. A talon ripped through the sleeve, and the sleeve fell away. At the same time the heavy stick caught the eagle across its open wing. The bird gave a shrill cry of pain and fury. Then it turned and flapped heavily away, flying unsteadily because of its injured wing.

Jai still clutched the stick, because he expected the bird to return; he did not even glance at his torn jacket. But the golden eagle had alighted on a distant rock and was in no hurry to return to the attack.

Jai began driving the sheep home. The clouds had become heavy and black, and presently the first snow-flakes began to fall.

Jai saw a hare go lolloping down the hill. When it was about fifty yards away, there was a rush of air from the eagle's beating wings, and Jai saw the bird approaching the hare in a sidelong drive.

'So it hasn't been badly hurt,' thought Jai, feeling a little relieved, for he could not help admiring the great bird. 'Now it has found something else to chase for its dinner.'

The hare saw the eagle and dodged about, making for a clump of junipers. Jai did not know if it was caught or not, because the snow and sleet had increased and both bird and hare were lost in the gathering snow-storm.

The sheep were bleating behind him. One of the lambs looked tired, and he stooped to pick it up. As he did so, he heard a thin, whining sound. It grew louder by the second. Before he could look up, a huge wing caught him across the shoulders and sent him sprawling. The lamb tumbled down the slope with him, into a thorny bilberry bush.

The bush saved them. Jai saw the eagle coming in again, flying low. It was another eagle! One had been vanquished, and now here was another, just as big and fearless, probably the mate of the first eagle.

Jai had lost his stick and there was no way in which he could fight the second eagle. So he crept further into the bush, holding the lamb beneath him. At the same time he began shouting at the top of his voice—both to scare the bird away and to summon help. The eagle could not easily get at them now; but the rest of the flock was exposed on the hillside. Surely the eagle would make for them.

Even as the bird circled and came back in another dive, Jai heard fierce barking. The eagle immediately swung away and rose skywards.

The barking came from Motu. Hearing Jai's shouts and sensing that something was wrong, he had come limping out of the house, ready to do battle. Behind him came another shepherd and—most wonderful of all—Grandmother herself, banging two frying-pans together. The barking, the banging and the shouting frightened the eagles away. The sheep scattered too, and it was some time before they could all be rounded up. By then it was snowing heavily. 'Tomorrow we must all go down to Maku,' said the shepherd.

'Yes, it's time we went,' said Grandmother. 'You can read your story-books again, Jai.'

'I'll have my own story to tell,' said Jai.

When they reached the hut and Jai saw Grandfather, he said, 'Oh, I've forgotten your stick!'

But Motu had picked it up. Carrying it between his teeth, he brought it home and sat down with it in the open doorway. He had decided the cherry wood was good for his teeth and would have chewed it up if Grandmother hadn't taken it from him.

'Never mind,' said Grandfather, sitting up on his cot. 'It isn't the stick that matters. It's the person who holds it.'

THE TIGER AND THE TERRIER

Brig. General R.G. Burton

There was a time when 'griffins', as newcomers used to be called, expected to find tigers in their gardens and snakes in their boots when they went to India; but even thirty years ago such ideas were no longer prevalent, and were supposed to be found only in the tales of those eminent Anglo-Indians, Colonels Monsoon and Bowlong. But I was no novice when I arrived at a military cantonment in the Deccan in November 1898 and observed what a 'jungly' appearance it presented. Indeed, my first walk induced me to remark to my companion on the tigerish look of a nullah which ran through the place and was at that time overgrown with the luxuriant foliage of the rainy season.

But there were, so far as we knew, no tigers within a radius of fifty or sixty miles, and no jungles to hold them, although a tomb in the old cemetery recorded that an officer had been killed by one of these animals ten miles off about seventy years before this time. A tiger requires extensive jungles for its wanderings, and the country around us was now mostly under cultivation with some sparse bush and wasteland on the hills.

Yet, even then, all unknown to us, a tiger was padding his way towards the cantonment, and he had been seen, as I learnt long afterwards, by an old friend, a Muhammadan Mullah who was waiting in ambush for more harmless animals near a pool and whose heart 'turned to water' as he expressed it, at the sight of a monster such as he had never seen before. Leopards he was familiar with, for they were plentiful in his district twenty miles away, but the greatest cat of all was strange to him.

Adjoining the large compound in which my house stood was a garden some acres in extent containing a bungalow now empty, the dwelling place of a missionary who for many years did excellent and devoted work in the surrounding country. Here, in his absence a gardener was employed to keep the place in order. Only a day or two after my arrival from leave in England, the gardener came over to say that he had seen what he described as a leopard lying down in the veranda of the unoccupied bungalow. Such simple people are prone to exaggeration, and it was thought more probable that the animal was a wild or a large domestic cat. However, with a few followers and two sepoys we two turned out with our rifles, only to find the veranda empty. The gardener was, however, so sure that we decided to beat through an extensive patch of long grass in the compound, into which the animal must have retreated.

The two guns took up a position on the farther side of this patch while the men walked in line towards them. Suddenly, there was a rush and a roar, and not a leopard but a well-grown tiger, whose voice was at once recognizable, broke from the cover and sprang over the hedge, disappearing in a moment without giving the guns time to fire a shot. The tiger had made off as soon as it was disturbed, but in passing found time to strike down one of the sepoys and inflict some severe wounds on his back and shoulder. He was taken to hospital and made a good recovery in the course of a few weeks, although not in time to accompany us on the annual tiger-hunting expedition. No doubt, he had enough of tigers to last him the remainder of his life!

We then followed the tiger, which had disappeared in an adjoining compound. More 'guns' had arrived and we walked across the open accompanied by Sal, the bull-terrier, who soon turned the tiger out of a shallow nullah that ran along the hedge on one side of the compound. The animal fled, followed closely by the gallant Sal and by several bullets, fired to the danger of spectators in the vicinity. It was already growing dusk. The tiger had taken refuge in a deep and dense hedge, from which we tried in vain to dislodge it and in which it could not be seen. Darkness came on with the usual rapidity and suddenness. With the aid of lanterns we attempted to make out the lurking animal, but although we went up close and peered into the hedge, nothing could be seen. It was a situation not without danger, especially as the beast had probably been wounded and was certainly angry.

There was nothing to be done but to leave it until morning, when the tracks were taken up where they crossed the dusty road, one halting footmark showing that the tiger was going lame, as indicated also by a few drops of blood. It had evidently retreated soon after nightfall, and a mile farther on it had slaked its thirst at a pool in a nullah on the edge of the cantonment. It then made towards the low hills where the velvet-footed beast left no impression on the hard and stony ground. We beat through the surrounding country and day after day I rode many miles round in the direction taken by the tiger, but no trace of it was found until five days later when a man was seized in a field near a village six miles off; he was mortally wounded, his insides being almost torn out of his body. The unfortunate villager was able to speak, and before he died he related that he had been scaring birds in the *Jowari* {millet} when he heard a peculiar noise and on going towards the spot from which it came he was seized by the animal, which rushed out upon him.

We went to the scene of the tragedy which was in a field where the *jowari* grew to a height of six or seven feet. There we found the poor man's staff and cotton cloth, a pool of blood, and the tracks and a strong smell of the wild beast. We followed through the field and beyond, where the tracks were again lost on hard ground in a wide and rocky nullah. Dog Sal, though so keen and brave in the face of the enemy, seemed to have no nose for tracking.

We encamped upon the spot and next day beat through the nullahs in the neighbourhood without results. But the animal had to be killed. The whole country was in a panic, the people afraid to go out to work in the fields, and we feared to hear of more deaths, for the tiger, so far as we could ascertain, had taken no *prey*, and must be hungry and desperate; it is of such stuff that man-eaters are made. The district in which the animal had been lost sight of was hilly and broken, containing little water. It was obvious that it would have to find water to quench its thirst; even in normal conditions tigers are impatient of thirst, and doubly so when hunted and wounded. A mile or two across the hills we came to a nullah where there were fresh tracks, and we found a pool where the animal had watered; it was evidently lying up in the adjacent jungle.

We took post while Sal and the men beat through the cover, and the tiger soon broke and galloped across an open strip of ground pursued closely by the bull-terrier barking close at his heels. The chase disappeared in a patch of dense bush and after a succession of roars, howls, and barks Sal emerged, torn and bleeding from extensive wounds in the chest. Still the brave dog wanted to go in again and seek out her enemy, and had to be restrained.

Showers of stones and small shot failed to make the tiger move or give evidence of its situation. Night was coming on and we did not wish to leave it to another day which might involve a further prolonged chase and endanger more lives. Three of us, including a famous Indian officer who still resides near the scene of this encounter, crawled into the bush. After a long search we came suddenly upon the tiger which lay facing us, its eyes blazing in the gloom of the jungle, and appearing ready to charge, but a few shots put an end to its existence.

Poor old Sal was fat, heavy, and not very active, or she might have escaped the cruel claws; as it was she lived a fortnight, and eventually died of exhaustion when the wounds were already healing up. She was photographed with her bandages on the day before her death. The tiger was a male, probably between four and five years old and over eight feet in length. It had a wound which had splintered a bone above one of the hind feet, which showed signs of healing, but must have caused much pain and discomfort, no doubt sustained in the first encounter; there was a slight wound in the flank from a bullet fired when it was driven out on this last occasion, and the final shots were in the chest and the centre of the forehead, where the Subedar-Major's bullet had pierced the brain. The dead animal was carried back to the cantonment, where thousands assembled to view the bold beast which had given so much trouble, and which, they said, had come in search of one who had killed so many of its kind.

Mention has been made of snakes, which were exceedingly abundant in this part of the country. A krait one night left its skin on a teapoy at the bedside; Russell's vipers were numerous, and one that lay in the doorway of a bedroom was nearly trodden upon, but was fortunately betrayed by its loud and persistent hissing. So, tigers in gardens and snakes in bungalows are not only to be found in the tales of our old Indian officers, Bowlong and Monsoon, at any rate they were met with thirty years ago.

The cantonment where these episodes took place has been long since abandoned, and the echoes are forever silent which once resounded with the tramp of horse and foot and the thunder of guns. In those days the line of rail was nearly hundred miles distant. But should any now wish to travel to the scene of these and many other adventures, or to visit the battlefield where the greatest of English generals gained a famous victory, they need not traverse the long and dusty road along which the pony-tongas used to labour in days gone by. For, they can alight from the train within a mile of the spot where the invading tiger lay up on that November day.

TOOMAI OF THE ELEPHANTS

Rudyard Kipling

I will remember what I was. I am sick of rope and chain,
I will remember my old strength and all my forest affairs.
I will not sell my back to man for a bundle of sugarcane,
I will go out to my own kind, and the wood folk in their lairs.

I will go out until the day, until the morning break,
Out to the winds' untainted kiss, the waters' clean caress:
I will forget my ankle-ring and snap my picket-stake,
I will revisit my lost loves, and playmates masterless!

Kala Nag, which means Black Snake, had served the Indian government in every way that an elephant could serve it for forty-seven years, and as he was fully twenty years old when he was caught, that makes him nearly seventy—a ripe age for an elephant. He remembered pushing, with a big leather pad on his forehead, at a gun stuck in deep mud, and that was before the Afghan War of 1842, and he had not then come to his full strength. His mother, Radha Pyari—Radha, the darling—who had been caught in the same drive with

Kala Nag, told him, before his little milk-tusks had dropped out, that elephants who were afraid always got hurt; and Kala Nag knew that the advice was good, for the first time that he saw a shell burst he backed, screaming, into a stand of piled rifles, and the bayonets pricked him in all his softest places. So, before he was twenty-five he gave up being afraid, and he was the best-loved and the best-looked-after elephant in the service of the Government of India. He had carried tents, twelve hundred pounds' weight of tents, on the march in Upper India; he had been hoisted into a ship at the end of a steam-crane and taken for days across the water, and made to carry a mortar on his back in a strange and rocky country very far from India, and had seen the Emperor Theodore lying dead in Magdala, and had come back again in the steamer, entitled, so the soldiers said, to the Abyssinian War Medal. He had seen his fellow-elephants die of cold and epilepsy and starvation and sunstroke up at a place called Ali Masjid, ten years later; and afterwards he had been sent down thousands of miles south to haul and pile big baulks of teak in the timber-yards at Moulmein. There, he had half-killed an insubordinate young elephant who was shirking his fair share of the work.

After that he was taken off timber-hauling, and employed, with a few score of other elephants who were trained to the business, in helping to catch wild elephants among the Garo hills. Elephants are very strictly preserved by the Indian government. There is one whole department which does nothing else but hunt for them, and catch them, and break them in, and send them up and down the country as they are needed for work.

Kala Nag stood ten fair feet at the shoulders, and his tusks had been cut off short at five feet, and bound round the ends, to prevent them from splitting, with bands of copper; but he could do more with those stumps than any untrained elephant could do with the real sharpened ones.

When, after weeks and weeks of cautious driving of scattered elephants across the hills, the forty or fifty wild monsters were driven into the last stockade, and the big drop-gate, made of tree-trunks lashed together, jarred down behind them, Kala Nag, at the word of command, would go into that flaring, trumpeting pandemonium (generally at night, when the flicker of the torches made it difficult to judge distances), and, picking out the biggest and wildest tusker of the mob, would hammer him and hustle him into quiet while the men on the backs of the ether elephants roped and tied the smaller ones.

There was nothing in the way of fighting that Kala Nag, the old wise Black Snake, did not know for he had stood up more than once in his time to the charge of the wounded tiger, and, curling up his soft trunk to be out of harm's way, had knocked the springing brute sideways in mid-air with a quick sickle-cut of his head, that he had invented all by himself; had knocked him over, and kneeled upon him with his huge knees till the life went out with a gasp and a howl; and there was only a fluffy striped thing on the ground for Kala Nag to pull by the tail.

'Yes,' said Big Toomai, his driver, the son of Black Toomai who had taken him to Abyssinia, and grandson of Toomai of the Elephants who had seen him caught, there is nothing that the Black Snake fears except me. He has seen three generations of us feed him and groom him, and he will live to see four.'

'He is afraid of *me* also,' said Little Toomai, standing up to his full height of four feet, with only one rag upon him. He was ten years old, the eldest son of Big Toomai, and, according to custom, he would take his father's place on Kala Nag's neck when he grew up, and would handle the heavy iron ankus, the elephant-goad that had been worn smooth by his father, and his grandfather, and his great-grandfather. He knew what he was talking of; for he had been born under Kala Nag's shadow, had played with the end of his trunk before he could walk, had taken him down to water as soon as he could walk, and Kala Nag would no more have dreamed of disobeying his shrill little orders than he would have dreamed of killing him on that day when Big Toomai carried the little brown baby under Kala Nag's tusks, and told him to salute his master that was to be.

'Yes,' said Little Toomai, 'he is afraid of *me*; and he took long strides up to Kala Nag, called him a fat old pig, and made him lift up his feet one after the other.'

'Wah!' said Little Toomai, 'thou art a big elephant' and he wagged his fluffy head, quoting his father. 'The Government may pay for elephants, but they belong to us mahouts. When thou art old, Kala Nag, there will come some rich Rajah, and he will buy thee from the Government, on account of thy size and thy manners, and then thou wilt have nothing to do but to carry gold earrings in thy ears, and a gold howdah on thy back, and a red cloth covered with gold on thy sides, and walk at the head of the processions of the King. Then, I shall sit on thy neck, O Kala Nag, with a silver ankus, and men will run before us with golden sticks, crying, "Room for the King's elephant!: That will be good, Kala Nag, but not so good as this hunting in the jungles.'

'Umph!' said Big Toomai. 'Thou art a boy, and as wild as a buffalo-calf. This running up and down among the hills is not the best Government service. I am getting old, and I do not love wild elephants. Give me brick elephant-lines, one stall to each elephant, and big stumps to tie them to safely, and flat, broad roads to exercise upon, instead of this come-and-go camping. Aha, the Cawnpore barracks were good. There was a bazaar close by, and only three hours' work a day.'

Little Toomai remembered the Cawnpore elephant-lines and said nothing. He very much preferred the camp life, and hated those broad, flat roads, with the daily grubbing for grass in the forage-reserve, and the long hours when there was nothing to do except to watch Kala Nag fidgeting in his pickets.

What Little Toomai liked was the scramble up bridle-paths that only an elephant could take; the dip into the valley below; the glimpses of the wild elephants browzing miles away; the rush of the frightened pig and peacock under Kala Nag's feet; the blinding warm rains, when all the hills and valleys smoked; the beautiful misty mornings when nobody knew where they would camp that night; the steady, cautious drive of the wild elephants, and the mad rush and blaze and hullabaloo of the last night's drive, when the elephants poured into the stockade like boulders in a landslide, found that they could not get out, and flung themselves at the heavy posts only to be driven back by yells and flaring torches and volleys of blank cartridge.

Even a little boy could be of use there, and Toomai was as useful as three boys. He would get his torch and wave it, and yell with the best. But the really good time came when the driving out began, and the *Keddah*—that is, the stockade—looked like a picture of the end of the world, and men had to make signs to one another, because they could not hear themselves speak. Then, Little Toomai would climb up to the top of one of the quivering stockade-posts, his sun-bleached brown hair flying loose all over his shoulders, and he looking like a goblin in the torch-light; and as soon as there was a lull you could hear his high-pitched yells of encouragement to Kala Nag, above the trumpeting and crashing, and snapping of ropes, and groans of the tethered elephants. *'Mail, mail, Kala Nag!* (Go on, go on, Black Snake!) *Dant do!* (Give him the tusk!) *Somalo! Somalo!* (Careful, careful!) *Maro! Maro!* (Hit him, hit him!) Mind the post! *Arre! Arre! Hai! Yai! Kya-a-ah!*' he would shout, and the big fight between Kala Nag and the wild elephant would sway to and fro across the Keddah, and the old elephant-catchers would wipe the sweat out of their eyes, and find time to nod to Little Toomai wriggling with joy on the top of the posts.

He did more than wriggle. One night, he slid down from the post and slipped in between the elephants, and threw up the loose end of a rope, which had dropped, to a driver who was trying to get a purchase on the leg of a kicking young calf (calves always give more trouble than full-grown animals). Kala Nag saw him, caught him in his trunk, and handed him up to Big Toomai, who slapped him then and there, and put him back on the post.

Next morning he gave him a scolding, and said: 'Are not good brick elephant-lines and a little tent-carrying enough, that thou must needs go elephant-catching on thy own account, little worthless? Now those foolish hunters, whose pay is less than my pay, have spoken to Petersen Sahib of the matter. Little Toomai was frightened. He did not know much of white men, but Petersen Sahib was the greatest white man in the world to him. He was the head of all the Keddah operations—the man who caught all the elephants for the Government of India, and who knew more about the ways of elephants than any living man.

'What...what will happen?' said Little Toomai.

'Happen! the worst that can happen. Petersen Sahib is a madman. Else, why should he go hunting these wild devils? He may even require thee to be an elephant-catcher, to sleep anywhere in these fever-filled jungles, and at last lobe trampled to death in the Keddah. It is well that this nonsense ends safely. Next week the catching is over, and we of the plains are sent back to our stations. Then, we will march on smooth roads, and forget all this hunting. But, son, I am angry that thou shouldst meddle in the business that belongs to these dirty Assamese jungle-folk. Kala Nag will obey none but me, so I must go with him into the Keddah; but he is only a fighting elephant, and he does not help to rope them. So, I sit at my ease, as befits a mahout,—not a mere hunter,—a mahout, say, and a man who gets a pension at the end of his service. Is the family of Toomai of the Elephants to be trodden underfoot in the dirt of a Keddah? Bad one! Wicked one! Worthless son! Go and wash Kala Nag and attend to his ears, and see that there are no thorns in his feet; or else Petersen Sahib will surely catch thee and make thee a wild hunter—a follower of elephants' foot-tracks, a jungle-bear. Bah! Shame! Go!'

Little Toomai went off without saying a word, but he told Kala Nag all his grievances while he was examining his feet. 'No matter,' said Little Toomai, turning up the fringe of Kala Nag's huge right ear. 'They have sent my name to Petersen Sahib, and perhaps—and perhaps—and perhaps—who knows? Hai! That is a big thorn that I have pulled out!'

The next few days were spent in getting the elephants together, in walking the newly caught wild elephants up and down between a couple of tame ones, to prevent them from giving too much trouble on the downward march to the plains, and in taking stock of the blankets and ropes and things that had been worn out or lost in the forest.

Petersen Sahib came in on his clever she-elephant Pudmini. He had been paying off other camps among the hills, for the season was coming to an end, and there was a native clerk sitting at a table under a tree to pay the drivers their wages. As each man was paid he went back to his elephant, and joined the line that stood ready to start. The catchers, and hunters, and beaters, the men of the regular Keddah, who stayed in the jungle year in and year out, sat on the backs of the elephants that belonged to Petersen Sahib's permanent force, or leaned against the trees with their guns across their arms, and made fun of the drivers who were going away, and laughed when the newly caught elephants broke the line and ran about.

Big Toomai went up to the clerk with Little Toomai behind him, and Machua Appa, the head-tracker, said in an undertone to a friend of his, 'There goes one piece of good elephant-stuff at least. 'Tis a pity to send that young jungle-cock to moult in the plains.'

Now Petersen Sahib had ears all over him, as a man must have who listens to the most silent of all living things—the wild elephant. He turned where he was lying all along on Pudmini's back, and said, 'What is that? I did not know of a man among the plains-drivers who had wit enough to rope even a dead elephant.'

'This is not a man, but a boy. He went into the Keddah at the last drive, and threw Barmao there the rope when we were trying to get that young calf with the blotch on his shoulder away from his mother!'

Machua Appa pointed at Little Toomai, and Petersen Sahib looked, and Little Toomai bowed to the earth.

'He threw a rope? He is smaller than a picket-pin. Little one, what is thy name?' said Petersen Sahib.

Little Toomai was too frightened to speak, but Kala Nag was behind him, and Toomai made a sign with his hand, and the elephant caught him up in his trunk and held him level with Pudmini's forehead, in front of the great Petersen Sahib.

Then, Little Toomai covered his face with his hands, for he was only a child, and except where elephants were concerned, be was just as bashful as a child could be.

'Oho!' said Petersen Sahib, smiling underneath his moustache, 'and why didst thou teach thy elephant *that* trick? Was it to help thee steal green corn from the roofs of the houses when the ears are put out to dry?

'Not green corn, Protector of the Poor—melons,' said Little Toomai, and all the men sitting about broke into a roar of laughter. Most of them had taught their elephants that trick when they were boys. Little Toomai was hanging eight feet up in the air, and he wished very much that he were eight feet under ground.

'He is Toomai, my son, Sahib,' said Big Toomai, scowling. 'He is a very bad boy, and he will end in a jail, Sahib.'

'Of that I have my doubts,' said Petersen Sahib. 'A boy who can face a full Keddah at his age does not end up in jails. See, little one, here are four annas to spend in sweetmeats because thou hast a little head under that great thatch of hair. In time thou mayest become a hunter, too.' Big Toomai scowled more than ever. 'Remember, though, that Keddahs are not good for children to play in,' Petersen Sahib went on.

'Must I never go there, Sahib?' asked Little Toomai, with a big gasp.

'Yes.' Petersen Sahib smiled again. 'When thou hast seen the elephants dance. That is the proper time. Come to me when thou hast seen the elephants dance, and then I will let thee go into all the Keddahs.'

There was another roar of laughter, for that is an old joke among elephant-catchers, and it means just never. There are great cleared flat places hidden away in the forests that are called elephants' ball-rooms, but even these are only found by accident, and no man has ever seen the elephants dance. When a driver boasts of his skill and bravery the other drivers say, 'And when didst *thou* see the elephants dance?'

Kala Nag put Little Toomai down, and he bowed to the earth again and went away with his father, and gave the silver four-*anna* piece to his mother, who was nursing his baby brother, and they all were put on Kala Nag's back, and the line of grunting, squealing elephants rolled down the hill-path to the plains. It was a very lively march on account of the new elephants, who gave trouble at every ford, and who needed coaxing or beating every other minute.

Big Toomai prodded Kala Nag spitefully, for he was very angry, but Little Toomai was too happy to speak. Petersen Sahib had noticed him, and given him money, so he felt as a private soldier would feel if he had been called out of the ranks and praised by his commander-in-chief.

'What did Petersen Sahib mean by the elephant-dance?' he said, at last, softly to his mother.

Big Toomai heard him and grunted. 'That thou shouldst never be one of these hill-buffaloes of trackers. *That* was what he meant. Oh, you in front, what is blocking the way?'

An Assamese driver, two or three elephants ahead, turned round angrily, crying: 'Bring up Kala Nag, and knock this youngster of mine into good behaviour. Why should Petersen Sahib have chosen *me* to go down with you donkeys of the rice-fields? Lay your beast alongside, Toomai, and let him prod with his tusks. By all the Gods of the Hills, these new elephants are possessed, or else they can smell their companions in the jungle.'

Kala Nag hit the new elephant in the ribs and knocked the wind out of him, as Big Toomai said, 'We have swept the hills of wild elephants at the last catch. It is only your carelessness in driving. Must I keep order along the whole line?'

'Hear him!' said the other driver. '*We* have swept the hills! Ho! ho! You are very wise, you plains-people. Anyone but a mud-head who never saw the jungle would know that *they* know that the drives are ended for the season. Therefore, all the wild elephants tonight will—but why should I waste wisdom on a river-turtle?'

'What will they do?' Little Toomai called out.

'*Ohé*, little one. Art thou there? Well, I will tell thee, for thou hast a cool head. *They* will dance, and it behoves thy father, who has swept *all* the hills of *all* the elephants, to double-chain his pickets tonight.'

'What talk is this?' said Big Toomai. 'For forty years, father and son, we have tended elephants, and we have never heard such moonshine about dances.'

'Yes; but a plains-man who lives in a hut knows only the four walls of his hut. Well, leave thy elephants unshackled tonight and see what comes; as for their dancing, I have seen the place where—*Bapree-Bap!* how many windings has the Dihang River? Here is another ford, and we must swim the calves. Stop still, you behind there.'

And in this way, talking and wrangling and splashing through the rivers, they made their first march to a sort of receiving-camp for the new elephants; but they lost their tempers long before they got there.

Then, the elephants were chained by their hind legs to their big stumps of pickets, and extra ropes were fitted to the new elephants, and the fodder was piled before them, and the hill-drivers went back to Petersen Sahib through the afternoon light, telling the plains-drivers to be extra careful that night, and laughing when the plains-drivers asked the reason.

Little Toomai attended to Kala Nag's supper, and as evening

fell wandered through the camp, unspeakably happy, in search of a tom-tom. When an Indian child's heart is full, he does not run about and make a noise in an irregular fashion. He sits down to a sort of revel all by himself. And Little Toomai had been spoken to by Petersen Sahib! If he had not found what he wanted, I believe he would have burst. But the sweetmeat-seller in the camp lent him a little tom-tom—a drum beaten with the flat of the hand—and he sat down, cross-legged, before Kala Nag as the stars began to come out, the tom-tom in his lap, and he thumped and he thumped and he thumped, and the more he thought of the great honour that had been done to him, the more he thumped, all alone among the elephant-fodder. There was no tune and no words, but the thumping made him happy.

The new elephants strained at their ropes, and squealed and trumpeted from time to time, and he could hear his mother in the camp hut putting his small brother to sleep with an old, old song about the great God Shiv, who once told all the animals what they should eat. It is a very soothing lullaby, and the first verse says:

> Shiv, who poured the harvest and made the winds to blow,
> Sitting at the doorways of a day of long ago.
> Gave to each his portion, food and toil and fate,
> From the King upon the guddee to the Beggar at the gate.
> All things made he—Shiva the Preserver.
> Mahadeo! Mahadeo! He made all,—
> Thorn for the camel, fodder for the kine.
> And mother's heart for sleepy head, O little son of mine!

Little Toomai came in with a joyous *tunk-a-tunk* at the end of each verse, till he felt sleepy and stretched himself on the fodder at Kala Nag's side.

At last, the elephants began to lie down one after another, as is their custom, till only Kala Nag at the right of the line was left standing up; and he rocked slowly from side-to-side, his ears put forward to listen to the night wind as it blew very slowly across the hills. The air was full of all the night noises that, taken together, make one big silence—the click of one bamboo-stem against the other, the rustle of something alive in the undergrowth, the scratch and squawk of a half-waked bird (birds are awake in the night much more often than we imagine), and the fall of water ever so far away. Little Toomai slept for some time, and when he waked it was brilliant moonlight, and Kala Nag was still standing up with his ears cocked. Little Toomai turned, rustling in the fodder, and watched the curve of his big back against half the stars in heaven; and while he watched he heard, so far away that it sounded no more than a pinhole of noise pricked through the stillness, the 'hoot-toot' of a wild elephant.

All the elephants in the lines jumped up as if they had been shot, and their grunts at last woke the sleeping mahouts, and they came out and drove in the picket-pegs with big mallets, and tightened this rope and knotted that till all was quiet. One new elephant had nearly grubbed up his picket, and Big Toomai took off Kala Nag's leg-chain and shackled that elephant fore-foot to hind-foot, but slipped a loop of grass-string round Kala Nag's leg, and told him to remember that he was tied fast. He knew that he and his father and his grandfather had done the very same thing hundreds of times before. Kala Nag did not answer to the order by gurgling, as he usually did. He stood still, looking out across the moonlight, his head a little raised, and his ears spread like fans, up to the great folds of the Garo Hills.

'Look to him if he grows restless in the night,' said Big Toomai to Little Tooinai, and he went into the hut and slept. Little Toomai was just going to sleep, too, when he heard the coir string snap with a little 'tang' and Kala Nag rolled out of his pickets as slowly and as silently as a cloud rolls out of the mouth of a valley. Little Toomai pattered after him, barefooted, down the road in the moonlight, calling under his breath, 'Kala Nag! Kala Nag! Take me with you, O Kala Nag!' The elephant turned without a sound, took three strides back to the boy in the moonlight, put down his trunk, swung him up to his neck, and almost before Little Toomai had settled his knees slipped into the forest.

There was one blast of furious trumpeting from the lines, and then the silence shut down on everything, and Kala Nag began to move. Sometimes, a tuft of high grass washed along his sides as a wave washes along the sides of a ship, and sometimes a cluster of wild-pepper vines would scrape along his back, or a bamboo would creak where his shoulder touched it; but between those times he moved absolutely without any sound, drifting through the thick Garo forest as though it had been smoke. He was going uphill, but though Little Toomai watched the stars in the rifts of the trees, he could not tell in what direction.

Then, Kala Nag reached the crest of the ascent and stopped for a minute, and Little Toomai could see the tops of the trees lying all speckled and furry under the moonlight for miles and miles, and the blue-white mist over the river in the hollow. Toomai leaned forward and looked, and he felt that the forest was awake below him—awake and alive and crowded. A big brown fruit-eating bat brushed past his ear; a porcupine's quills rattled in the thicket; and in the darkness between the tree-stems he heard a hog-bear digging hard in the moist, warm earth, and snuffing as it digged.

Then, the branches closed over his head again, and Kala Nag began to go slowly down into the valley—not quietly this time, but as a runaway gun goes down a steep bank—in one rush. The huge limbs moved as steadily as pistons, eight feet to each stride, and the wrinkled skin of the elbow-points rustled. The undergrowth on either side of him ripped with a noise like torn canvas, and the saplings that he heaved away right and left with his shoulders sprang back again, and banged him on the flank, and great trails of creepers, all matted together, hung from his tusks as he threw his head from side-to-side and ploughed out his pathway. Then, Little Toomai laid himself down close to the great neck, lest a swinging bough should sweep him to the ground, and he wished that he were back in the lines again.

The grass began to get squashy, and Kala Nag's feet sucked and squelched as he put them down, and the night mist at the bottom of the valley chilled Little Toomai. There was a splash and a trample, and the rush of running water, and Kala Nag strode through the bed of a river, feeling his way at each step. Above the noise of the water, as it swirled round the elephant's legs, Little Tooinai could hear more splashing and some trumpeting both up stream and down—great grunts and angry snortings, and all the mist about him seemed to be full of rolling, wavy shadows.

'*Ai!*' he said, half-aloud, his teeth chattering. 'The elephant-folk out tonight, it is the dance, then.'

Kala Nag swashed out of the water, blew his trunk clear, and began another climb; but this time he was not alone, and he had not to make his path. 'That was made already, six feet wide, in front of him, where the bent jungle-grass was trying to recover itself and stand up. Many elephants must have gone that way only a few minutes before. Little Toonmai looked back, and behind him a great wild tusker, with his little pig's eyes glowing like hot coals, was just lifting himself out of the misty river. Then the trees closed up again, and they went on and up, with trumpetings and crashings, and the sound of breaking branches on every side of them.

At last, Kala Nag stood still between two tree-trunks at the very top of the hill. They were part of a circle of trees that grew round an irregular space of some three or four acres, and in all that space, as Little Toormai could see, the ground had been trampled down as hard as a brick floor. Some trees grew in the centre of the clearing, but their bark was rubbed away, and the white wood beneath showed all shiny and polished in the patches of moonlight. There were creepers hanging from the upper branches, and the bells of the flowers of the creepers, great waxy white things like convolvuluses, hung down fast asleep; but within the limits of the clearing there was not a single blade of green—nothing but the trampled earth.

The moonlight showed it all iron-grey, except where some elephants stood upon it, and their shadows were inky black. Little Toomai looked, holding his breath, with his eyes starting out of his head, and as he looked, more and more and more elephants swung out into the open from between the tree-trunks. Little Toomai could count only up to ten, and he counted again and again on his fingers till he lost count of the tens, and his head began to swim. Outside the clearing he could hear them crashing in the undergrowth as they worked their way up the hillside; but as soon as they were within the circle of the tree-trunks they moved like ghosts.

There were white-tusked wild ones, with fallen leaves and nuts and twigs lying in the 'wrinkles of their necks and the folds of their ears; fat, slow-footed she-elephants, with restless little pinky black calves only three or four feet high running under their stomachs; young elephants with their tusks just beginning to show, and very proud of them; lanky, scraggy old-maid elephants, with their hollow, anxious faces, and trunks like rough bark; savage old bull-elephants, scarred from shoulder to flank with great weals and cuts of bygone fights, and the caked dirt of their solitary mud-baths dropping from their shoulders; and there was one with a broken tusk and the marks of the full-stroke, the terrible drawing scrape, of a tigers claws on his side.

They were standing head to head, or walking to and fro across the ground in couples, or rocking and swaying all by themselves—scores and scores of elephants.

Toomai knew that, so long as he lay still on Kala Nag's neck, nothing would happen to him; for even in the rush and scramble of a Keddah-drive a wild elephant does not reach up with his trunk and drag a man off the neck of a tame elephant; and these elephants were not thinking of men that night. Once they started and put their ears forward when they heard the chinking of a leg-iron in the forest, but it was Pudmini, Petersen Sahib's pet elephant, her chain snapped short off, grunting, snuffling up the hillside. She must have broken her pickets, and come straight from Petersen Sahib's camp; and Little Toomai saw another elephant, one that he did not know, with deep rope-galls on his back and breast. He, too, must have run away from some camp in the hills about.

At last, there was no sound of any more elephants moving in the forest, and Kala Nag rolled out from his station between the trees and went into the middle of the crowd, clucking and gurgling, and all the elephants began to talk in their own tongue, and to move about.

Still lying down, Little Toomai looked down upon scores

and scores of broad backs, and wagging ears, and tossing trunks, and little rolling eyes. He heard the click of tusks as they crossed other tusks by accident, and the dry rustle of trunks twined together, and the chafing of enormous sides and shoulders in the crowd, and the incessant flick and *hissh* of the great tails. Then, a cloud came over the moon, and he sat in black darkness; but the quiet, steady hustling and pushing and gurgling went on just the same. He knew that there were elephants all around Kala Nag, and that there was no chance of backing him out of the assembly; so he set his teeth and shivered. In a Keddah at least there was torchlight and shouting, but here he was all alone in the dark, and once a trunk came up and touched him on the knee.

Then an elephant trumpeted, and they all took it up for five or ten terrible seconds. The dew from the trees above spattered down like rain on the unseen backs, and a dull booming noise began, not very loud at first, and Little Toomai could not tell what it was; but it grew and grew, and Kala Nag lifted up one fore-foot and then the other, and brought them down on the ground—one-two, one-two, as steadily as trip-hammers. The elephants were stamping all together now and it sounded like a war-drum beaten at the mouth of a cave. The dew fell from the trees till there was no more left to fall, and the booming went on, and the ground rocked and shivered, and Little Toomai put his hands to his ears to, shut out the sound. But it was all one gigantic jar that ran through him—this stamp of hundreds of heavy feet on the raw earth. Once or twice he could feel Kala Nag and all the others surge forward a few strides, and the thumping would change to the crushing sound of juicy green things being bruised, but in a minute or two the boom of feet on hard earth began again. A tree was creaking and groaning somewhere near him. He put out his arm and felt the bark, but Kala Nag moved forward, still tramping, and he could not tell where he was in the clearing. There was no sound from the elephants, except once, when two or three little calves squeaked together. Then he heard a thump and a shuffle, and the booming went on. It must have lasted fully two hours, and Little Toomai ached in every nerve; but he knew by the smell of the night air that the dawn was conning.

The morning broke in one sheet of pale yellow behind the green hills, and the booming stopped with the first ray, as though the light had been an order. Before Little Toomai had got the ringing out of his head, before even he had shifted his position, there was not an elephant in sight except Kala Nag, Pudmini, and the elephant with the rope-galls, and there was neither sign nor rustle nor whisper down the hillsides to show where the others had gone.

Little Toomai stared again and again. The clearing, as he remembered it, had grown in the night. More trees stood in the middle of it, but the undergrowth and the jungle-grass at the sides bad been rolled back. Little Toomai stared once more. Now, he understood the trampling. The elephants had stamped out more room—had stamped the thick grass and juicy cane to trash, the trash into slivers, the slivers into tiny fibres, and the fibres into hard earth.

'Wah!' said Little Toomai, and his eyes were very heavy. 'Kala Nag, my lord, let us keep by Pudmini and go to Petersen Sahib's camp, or I shall drop from thy neck.'

The third elephant watched the two go away, snorted, wheeled round, and took his own path. He may have belonged to some little native king's establishment, fifty or sixty or a hundred miles away.

Two hours later, as Petersen Sahib was eating early breakfast, the elephants, who had been double-chained that night, began to trumpet, and Pudmini, mired to the shoulders, with Kala Nag, very foot-sore, shambled into the camp.

Little Toomai's face was grey and pinched, and his hair was full of leaves and drenched with dew; but he tried to salute Petersen Sahib, and cried faintly: 'The dance—the elephant-dance! I have seen it, and—I did!' As Kala Nag sat down, he slid off his neck in a dead faint.

But, since native children have no nerves worth speaking of, in two hours he was lying very contentedly in Petersen Sahib's hammock with Petersen Sahib's shooting-coat under his head, and a glass of warm milk, a little brandy, with a dash of quinine inside of him; and while the old hairy, scarred hunters of the jungles sat three-deep before him, looking at him as though he were a spirit, he told his tale in short words, as a child will, and wound up with:

'Now, if I lie in one word, send men to see, and they will find that the elephant-folk have trampled down more room in their dance-room, and they will find ten and ten, and many times ten, tracks leading to that dance-room. They made more room with their feet, I have seen it. Kala Nag took me, and I saw. Also, Kala Nag is very leg-weary!'

Little Toomai lay back and slept all through the long afternoon and into the twilight, and while he slept Petersen Sahib and Machua Appa followed the track of the two elephants for fifteen miles across the hills. Petersen Sahib had spent eighteen years in catching elephants, and he had only once before found such a dance-place. Machua Appa had no need to look twice at the clearing to see what had been done there, or to scratch with his toe in the packed, rammed earth.

'The child speaks truth,' said he. 'All this was done last night, and I have counted seventy tracks: crossing the river. See, Sahib, where Pudmini's leg-iron cut the bark off that tree!

Yes; she was there, too.'

They looked at each other, and up and down, and they wondered; for the ways of elephants are beyond the wit of any, man, black or white, to fathom.

'Forty years and five,' said Machua Appa, 'have I followed my lord the elephant, but never have I heard that any child of man had seen what this child has seen, By all the Gods of the Hills, it is what can we say?' and he shook his head.

When they got back to camp it was time for the evening meal. Petersen Sahib ate alone in his tent, but he gave orders that the camp should have two sheep and some fowls, as well as a double ration of flour and rice and salt, for he knew that there would be a feast.

Big Toomai had come up hot-foot from the camp in the plains to search for his son and his elephant, and now that he had found them he looked at them as though he were afraid of them both. And there was a feast by the blazing camp-fires in front of the lines of picketed elephants, and Little Toomai was the hero of it all; and the big brown elephant-catchers, the trackers and drivers and ropers, and the men who know all the secrets of breaking the wildest elephants, passed him from one to the other, and they marked his forehead with blood from the breast of a newly killed jungle-cock, to show that he was a forester, initiated and free of all the jungles.

And at last, when the flames died down, and the red light of the logs made the elephants look as though they had been dipped in blood too, Machua Appa, the head of all the drivers of all the Keddahs,—Machua Appa, Petersen Sahib's other self, who had never seen a made road in forty years: Machua Appa, who was so great that he had no other name than Machua Appa,—leaped to his feet, with Little Toomai held high in the air above his head, and shouted: 'Listen, my brothers. Listen, too, you my lords in the lines there, for I, Machua Appa, am speaking! This little one shall no more be called Little Toomai, but Toomai of the Elephants, as his great-grandfather was called before him. What never man has seen he has seen through the long night, and the favour of the elephant-folk and of the Gods of the jungles is with him. He shall become a great tracker; he shall become greater than I, even I—Machua Appa! He shall follow the new trail, and the stale trail, and the mixed trail, with a clear eye! He shall take no harm in the Keddah when he runs under their bellies to rope the wild tuskers; and if he slips before the feet of the charging bull-elephant, that bull-elephant shall know who he is and shall not crush him. Aihai! my lords in the chains,'— he whirled up the line of pickets,—'here is the little one that has seen your dances in your hidden places—the sight that never man saw! Give him honour, my lords! *Salaam kayo,* my children! Make your salute to Toomai of the Elephants! Gunga Pershad, ahaa! Hira Guj, Birchi Guj, Kuttar Guj, ahaa! Pudmini,—thou hast seen him at the dance, and thou too, Kala Nag, my pearl among elephants!—Ahaa! Together! To Toomai of the Elephants. *Barrao!*'

And at that last wild yell the whole line flung up their trunks till the tips touched their foreheads, and broke out into the full salute, the crashing trumpet-peal that only the Viceroy of India hears—the Salaam-ut of the Keddah.

But it was all for the sake of Little Toomai, who had seen what never man had seen before—the dance of the elephants at night and alone in the heart of the Garo hills!

From *The Jungle Book*

DOWN ELEPHANT STREET

K.M. Eady

Maclaren was having his first experience of jungle marching, and, although Punch, when a little fellow, had seen something of that sort of work, it had never been through such tangle as this.

The forest trees, densely matted overhead, and each, in its turn, overgrown with thick masses of orchids and other creepers, so that the monkeys could race from tree-top to tree-top without a break, shut out the light of the sun and the cooling breezes from the human wayfarers below, while beneath, in the damp, stifling, oppressive heat, there seemed to be every kind of shrub and creeper that Nature could produce, capable of growing a thorn or sharp, sword-edged leaf to tear and wound the unwary passer-by.

The two lads made very slow progress, but that was only to be expected; the worst feature of the case was that it was by no means sure. They had no compass, they could not see the sun, and, in the soft, dim twilight of the forest, all paths—or rather, absence of paths—looked the same. After some time a vague, fear began to oppress Punch that they might not be keeping their course correctly, and he was 'considerably upset to find that Maclaren shared his fears, but their dismay was complete when, one evening, they came back to their last night's resting-place, and discovered that the day's march had been in a circle.

Both lads flung themselves down on the ground, and looked at each other in speechless dread. At length Punch spoke, 'A whole day lost!' he groaned, 'and perhaps that fellow Ismail close behind us!'

And, this may not be the first day that we've done the same thing, Maclaren added, still more dejectedly.

'And, it may tot be the last,' Punch suggested with a gasp.

'Oh! hang it, old fellow, now we know, we shall be able to prevent it,' Maclaren interposed hastily. 'We must fix on some big tree ahead, and keep straight on, and—'

'But that's what we have been trying to do all the time! Don't you see, old fellow, we can only see the trees a few yards ahead of us, and, when we reach one mark, we can't be sure that the next one is really straight ahead.

This was, unfortunately, only, too true, as many a traveller had discovered before them. They discussed the matter at length before settling down to rest, but could find no real solution to their difficulty. They resolved to be more careful, to mark each distinct clump of trees in their hinds as they passed, and, for the rest, to push on steadily and hope for the best, but it was with considerable misgiving that they started once more.

They dared not stray into the jungle in pursuit of game, but a continuous vegetable diet, and that a very sparing one, became exceedingly monotonous. When a herd crossed their path, or a single animal started up from under their feet, they were able now and again to spear a little wild pig, and once managed to secure one of the pretty little hogdeer which Maclaren had never seen before; but they always felt that the lighting of a fire, even in this dense forest, was dangerous work, and might bring their human enemies on them, while the scent of blood might attract other, and equally undesirable foes. Indeed, one night, when a portion of cooked hog's meat had been put aside, well wrapped in leaves, for the morrow, it was found to have been carried away by some noiseless visitor, and it was only by the tracks on the soft ground that the lads could gather how great a risk they had run of being mauled or killed.

But they were fated to pass through a far worse danger than this. One day, they had been making their way as usual through dense jungle, from time to time obliged to cut a path through the thicket of underwood and trailing creepers, and seeing only a few yards ahead into the dim recesses of the dark, silent forest. Suddenly Punch, who was leading, stopped short, and peered through the bushes at some unusual sight.

'What is it?' Maclaren whispered, coming to his side.

'A clearing. Look-straight ahead; and he pointed through the trees to where unmistakably a clearing had been made, not only in the underwood, but among the lesser trees.

'Is it those dwarf fellows again, or—or Malays,' and Maclaren's whisper betrayed his anxiety.

'I don't know; neither, I think. We have heard no axes, and, see—that tree has been uprooted, not cut down! Come on very carefully, and we'll spy out the land.'

With extreme caution they stole on, skirting the open space for fear of ambushed foes, but seeking for some spot where, themselves sheltered, they could view the clearing more closely. At length one was found, and then, leaning forward over the branch of a tree on its outskirts, the opening could be clearly observed.

It covered a considerable space, but appeared to have been roughly made, for its boundaries were uneven, and the trees and shrubs had been selected from all spots and of all kinds, and had been thrown down, singly or in heaps, in the wildest confusion. Some were strong young saplings, torn up bodily by the roots, tree ferns were pushed down, and pressed and broken into a heap of crushed bushes, and all the lower and smaller growth, had been trodden down into the miry ground below, which again was full of the marks of huge footsteps. Beyond, on the one side, a broad lane of broken and down-trodden shrubs showed whence the intruders had come, while another broad lane, nearly opposite, marked the spot of their exit, and, throughout both, lopped branches and torn down creepers, half-eaten and then thrown away, told their own tale of destruction, apparently quite as much for amusement as for food.

Punch laughed aloud, and sprang out fearlessly into the opening. 'Elephants,' he said reassuringly, as his companion followed him more cautiously. 'They've gone on, hours ago, after making hay very considerably here. There must have been a lot of them,' he added, as he tried to distinguish the footmarks.

'Elephants!' Maclaren repeated. 'Do you mean to say that they can make a clearing like this? Why, it would take a small army of woodmen to cut down all those trees.'

'No doubt, but it's child's play to a hungry elephant to haul up a tree, for the sake of a few leaves on its crown, perhaps. They're queer beasts. They seem to delight in smashing things about just for the fun of it. Look, some of those trees haven't been touched for food.'

'I wish we had been here earlier and could have seen them,'

Maclaren said eagerly. 'A herd of wild elephants very much at home in the jungle would have been a sight worth seeing.'

'Yes, *if* we had a couple of good rifles and were dead shots,' Punch replied with unusual gravity. 'As it is, the less we see of them the better. If we came across them and scared them, especially if there were any old cow elephants with young calves among them, they would charge like a shot, and'—he looked round expressively at the mass of destruction at their feet—'you can guess pretty well how we should come out of the business.'

'H'm!' Maclaren's sporting aspirations died away suddenly.

'Yes, they would make hay, as you call it, of us very easily. So, I suppose we mustn't use that road over there which they have so kindly made for us.'

'I don't know about that,' Punch replied doubtfully. 'They passed some time ago, and may have gone miles ahead by this time; on the other hand, they may be feeding or sleeping close by. They sleep a good deal in the daytime, I believe. Anyway, I think we may safely use their road for a bit, but we must keep a sharp look out, hold our tongues, tread softly, and, if we see or hear them, make for a big tree, and stay up in it until they move on. It wouldn't waste more time than cutting our way through this hateful jungle.'

'Don't abuse the jungle,' Maclaren laughed. 'It helped us out of Ismail's clutches.'

'We aren't out of the wood yet, literally or otherwise,' Punch replied, not very consolingly. 'Come on, old fellow, here goes for a trot down Elephant Street!'

It was certainly a relief to find a broad and comparatively smooth path prepared for them, and for some two miles or more it fed onwards in a fairly straight course, and, so far as the lads could judge, in the direction of Disting. So far, so good, but it was with considerable trepidation that both kept their eyes fixed steadily forward, looking ahead eagerly for new dangers. At length they reached as light incline, where the path led straight up to its summit, but, of course, beyond that point, further views, except of the thick wall of tree-tops below, were shut out by the hill itself. Very cautiously the lads stole up, endeavouring, with care learnt by experience, to avoid treading on dry twigs, or striking the boot against trunks or roots of trees.

They reached the top and looked down on a very curious sight. Below them lay a small, hollow, cup-shaped space, cleared, like the former opening, of all shrubs and smaller trees, and, among the litter of broken wood and disordered foliage, either asleep or lazily chewing the green food at their sides, lay a number of elephants. Several were large old tuskers, but, to Punch's dismay, he discerned among them two or three calves, and he knew that the mothers, always more vigilant than the males, would now be unusually watchful and fierce. If they should discover the presence of human beings, a charge was inevitable, and old stories, told him years before by European and native hunters, warned him of the extreme danger to themselves, practically unarmed as they were, of such a course:

He touched Maclaren on the shoulder, pointed to two big trees near the path, and sufficiently stout to withstand the charge of the strongest elephant, and made hurriedly but silently for one.

Maclaren followed him with equal haste and caution, but it was almost too late. Despite all their care, some sound must have been overheard, or perhaps the wind carried the scent of man—deadliest and most dreaded foe of all wild beasts—to some wakeful member of the slumbering herd, for, with a shrill scream of alarm, a huge, cow-elephant scrambled to her feet. The others followed her example, and for a moment all was confusion, before the herd closed up together, and stood, perfectly still, as though puzzling out the cause of the alarm. Then the first to move, forcing her way through the herd, threw up her trunk, and waved it in the air to catch the direction of the scent, then it was as rapidly drawn down, curled up, and she started to charge.

She came up the hill with almost incredible rapidity, and Maclaren, although most of his energies were devoted to the task of clambering up the tree trunk, regardless of prickly creepers and torn hands, face, and clothing, was yet able to observe, with considerable astonishment, the wonderful grace and dignity of the animal's movements. His former experience of elephants had been of domesticated beasts, performing various tasks in such a way as to exhibit them at their worst, their huge size and strength only increasing the awkwardness of their movements. But now, in her native forests, surrounded by giant vegetation, and moving in her silent wrath with great easy strides, very swiftly, but smoothly and regularly, there was something grand and majestic in this charge.

However, Maclaren had little time to notice all this, and to Punch, who had often before been an interested spectator at an elephant hunt, if not an actual hunter, there was nothing novel in the business, except the fact that the usual quarry was hunting the men, instead of the men hunting the elephant. He was already well up his tree, out of the reach of both tusks and trunk, and now turned anxiously to see how Maclaren was faring. But the sailor had not been equally fortunate. While he was still only some eight or ten feet from the ground the elephant sighted him, and, with another shrill snort of fury, prepared to charge.

Maclaren had not been at sea for six years for nothing. He caught at the branches above him with frantic haste, and hauled himself up with all possible speed, but even then he could not have got out of the way in time if Punch had not created a diversion in his favour.

The boy knew that it would be impossible to do serious damage to the huge brute with the poor weapon, a stout, iron-tipped, bamboo spear, which was all that he possessed, but he also knew how easily the anger of the elephant could be diverted for the time being, and he launched the spear with all his force against her great flapping ear. It sped truly and struck home, and the animal screamed once more with rage and pain, turned round, and charged straight at Punch's tree.

But here even her great strength could do little damage, for the great stern, although it rocked and creaked at each of her frantic charges, could have withstood greater *force* than she could bring to bear against it, and the boy was out of her reach, sitting astride a branch well above her head She soon realized this and returned to Maclaren, but he had taken advantage of the few moments' respite to climb as high as Punch himself, and, beyond a few splinters, and much swaying and groaning, his tree was none the worse for her attack.

The remainder of the herd had galloped away into the jungle, but from time to time came an appealing cry from her deserted calf, and at length the old elephant seemed weary of her fruitless attack. She looked from the one tree to the other, eyeing the two lads keenly with her little bright eyes, then, with one more angry scream, she dashed off to join her companions.

The danger was over for the present, but she might return, and the two young fellows thought it wise to remain for a considerable time in their leafy shelter. Then, at length, they ventured to descend and resume their march, but this time they preferred to take their own path, even at the risk of travelling once more in a circle.

From *Among Pirates and Pygmies*
by K.M. Eady (1897)